# Just for you

## Selfish Sewing with Your Favorite *SewCanShe* Bloggers

24 Simply Stylish Projects

Caroline Fairbanks-Critchfield and Sarah Markos

**stash** BOOKS.

*an imprint of C&T Publishing*

Text copyright © 2014 by Caroline Fairbanks-Critchfield and Sarah Markos

Photography and Artwork copyright © 2014 by C&T Publishing, Inc.

Publisher: Amy Marson

Creative Director: Gailen Runge

Art Director/Cover Designer: Kristy Zacharias

Editor: Lynn Koolish

Technical Editors: Debbie Rodgers and Mary E. Flynn

Book Designer: Casey Dukes

Production Coordinator/Illustrator: Jenny Davis

Production Editor: Katie Van Amburg

Photo Assistant: Mary Peyton Peppo

Styled photos by Nissa Brehmer, unless otherwise noted; Instructional photos by Diane Pedersen, unless otherwise noted

Published by Stash Books, an imprint of C&T Publishing, Inc., P.O. Box 1456, Lafayette, CA 94549

Library of Congress Cataloging-in-Publication Data

Fairbanks-Critchfield, Caroline, 1975-

 Just for you : selfish sewing with your favorite SewCanShe bloggers : 24 simply stylish projects / Caroline Fairbanks-Critchfield and Sarah Markos.
   pages cm
Collection of sewing projects by contributors to SewCanShe blog.
 ISBN 978-1-60705-907-3 (soft cover)
1.  Machine sewing. 2.  Tailoring--Patterns. 3.  Clothing and dress. 4.  Dress accessories.  I. Markos, Sarah, 1975- II. SewCanShe (Blog) III. Title.
 TT705.F35 2014
 646.2'044--dc23
                                                    2014008132

Printed in China

10 9 8 7 6 5 4 3 2 1

## DEDICATION

We dedicate this book to our mothers, fathers, grandmothers, and grandfathers, whose creativity, resourcefulness, and love of all things handmade inspired us to learn to sew.

## ACKNOWLEDGMENTS AND THANKS

First of all, we want to thank all of the talented sewists, designers, and bloggers who make up the amazing online sewing community. Without them, neither this book nor SewCanShe (sewcanshe.com) would be possible.

Second, we really must thank S. Truett Cathy, the founder of Chick-fil-A restaurants, for providing the perfect location for our weekly mommy-blogger business meetings. The ideas for this book first took shape while we sat in a Chick-fil-A booth drinking endless diet sodas as our preschoolers romped in the play area.

Third, we owe a debt of gratitude to our agent, Linda; to the tireless editors at C&T for answering our many questions and guiding us through our first book-writing experience; and to the very generous shops and manufacturers that provided the fabric and supplies needed for the projects and photographs in the book (see Where to Find It Online, page 128).

Thank you all. We are honored to call you our friends!

*Caroline and Sarah*

# Contents

# Introducing:
# A *SewCanShe* Book

Hello sewing fans! We are very excited to bring to you this collection of sewing projects written by many of our very favorite bloggers, with a few of our own designs as well.

Most of us spend our time sewing for our children, grandchildren, friends, and neighbors but hardly ever take the time to sew for ourselves. We want to make it easy for you to take occasional breaks from all of your *selfless* sewing and do some *selfish* sewing instead. We are giving you a challenge (and an excuse) to sew something for yourself every month of the year. The projects in this book are organized into twelve chapters for the twelve months of the year to keep you sewing sweet little projects all year long. You'll find clothing pieces, tote bags, purses, and accessories—all to make you feel spoiled.

Enjoy the beautiful pictures, reminiscent of a blog tutorial. We are sure you will find that in many cases a picture really does explain better than a thousand words. The projects in this book are written for sewists who have had some sewing experience but may still consider themselves beginners.

Be sure to check out Techniques You'll Use (page 120) for lots of tips (including how to make continuous bias trim) and a refresher of the things you'll need to know.

Let the Selfish Sewing begin!

# SWEETLY GATHERED ROUND HANDBAG

by Delia Randall

This chic, lightweight handbag features hand-made faux leather handles and lots of pocket options. The advantage of making your own handles is that they are more flexible to sew and more comfortable to wear. You may also use 8˝ premade hoop handles.

# MEET THE DESIGNER

Delia Randall is a 30-year-old mother to three beautiful children, a wife to a very patient husband, and an avid sewist who mostly enjoys sewing clothing for her children. She also likes to craft, crochet, and capture it all through her love of photography. She has a weakness for milkshakes, gardening, stripes, pretty fabric (especially striped pretty fabric), and kids who ask to be read to. You can read more about what Delia is currently sewing on her blog, *Delia Creates* (deliacreates.com).

---

**Finished size:** 16½″ wide × 13¼″ tall (without handles) × 6½″ deep

**Fabrics:** Yarn-Dyed Essex from Robert Kaufman and Waterfront Park by Violet Craft from Michael Miller Fabrics

---

## FABRIC REQUIREMENTS

- **For the outer bag:** ¾ yard of light- to midweight apparel fabric (at least 40″ wide)

- **For the lining:** 1⅛ yards of quilter's cotton or silky polyester (at least 40″ wide)

- **For the handles:** ¼ yard of faux leather or vinyl (55″–60″ wide) *Omit if using store-bought hoop handles.*

### Additional supplies

- **½″-wide upholstery cording:** 50″ (usually sold by the yard)

- **Leather and universal sewing machine needles**

- **Nylon zipper:** 7″ or longer

- **Hot-glue gun or masking tape**

> ## Delia's Tip
> If you are using store-bought hoop handles, you can omit the faux leather or vinyl. I found my vinyl in the home decor fabric clearance section of my fabric store. Many fabric stores also sell vinyl and faux leather on very tall rolls found near the clear vinyl or tablecloth vinyl section.

## CUTTING

✂ *Pattern is on pullout page P1.*

*From the vinyl, cut:*

2 strips 2½″ × 26½″

*Fold the outer fabric crosswise to a 13½″ × 40″ rectangle and cut:*

2 pieces using the Sweetly Gathered Handbag pattern, with the pattern placed on the fold

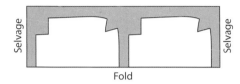

*Fold the lining fabric lengthwise 12″ from a selvage and cut:*

2 pieces using the Sweetly Gathered Handbag pattern, with the pattern placed on the fold

*From the single layer above the fold, cut:*

2 squares 10″ × 10″ for the welt zipper pocket

1 rectangle 11″ × 8″ for the divided pocket

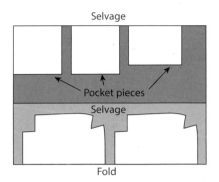

# Sewing

*Seam allowances are ½″ unless otherwise noted.*

## Sew the Zipper Welt Pocket

**1** Center 1 of the welt zipper pocket pieces in the middle of 1 of the lining pieces, right sides facing. Position it 4″ below the top of the notched side. Pin it at each corner. **A**

**2** Measure down 2″ from the top of the welt pocket piece. Using a ruler and a fabric-marking pen, draw a rectangle that is ½″ tall and 6″ wide. Draw a line down the middle vertically and horizontally. Draw two 45° lines from each corner. There will be 2 triangles at each end. Slide a pin through the vertical midline. **B**

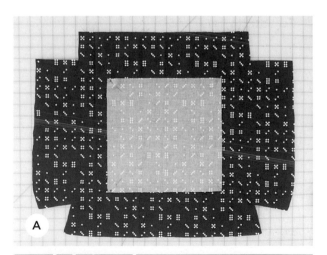

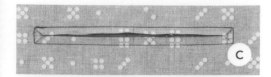

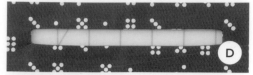

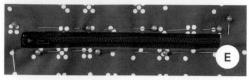

**3** Sew around the entire rectangle and cut along the middle line and triangles. Be sure not to clip any stitches. **C**

**4** Remove the pins and push the pocket piece through the cut hole to the wrong side. Press. If the corners are puckering, turn the pocket inside out again and clip closer to the corner without clipping a stitch. **D**

**5** Pin the zipper in place beneath the rectangle, with the zipper pull all the way to 1 side. **E**

**6** Topstitch around the rectangle, securing the zipper in place, sewing as close as possible to the zipper teeth on the ends (see Topstitching, page 126). Use a zipper foot or move the needle position if necessary. Trim the excess zipper. **F**

**7** Place the second welt pocket piece on top of the first pocket piece, right sides together, and pin it in place. Sew just the 2 pocket pieces together around all 4 edges. The raw edges will be encased between the bag lining and outer pieces and do not need to be finished. **G**

## Delia's Tip

I like to push the pins in with the heads away from the direction I will sew. That way I can remove the pins easily.

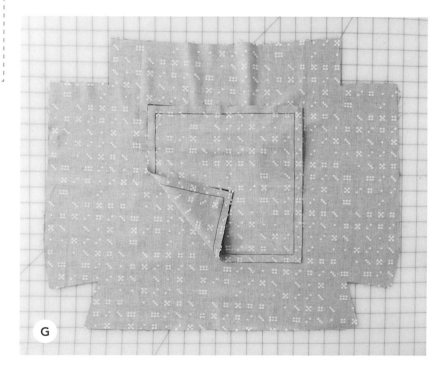

## Sew the Divided Pocket

**1** Fold the divided pocket piece in half, matching the short ends. Sew all the way around, leaving a 2″ opening on 1 of the sides. Trim the corners.

**2** Turn the pocket right side out. Use a dull pencil or a chopstick to push out the corners; then press.

**3** Place the pocket piece in the center of the other lining piece about 6″ down from the top, with the folded side at the top. Sew around the pocket close to the edges. Stitch a divider line down the middle, if desired.

## Make the Handles

**1** Cut the cording into 2 equal 25″ lengths. Tape the ends with masking tape before cutting to prevent fraying.

**2** Set the machine's stitch length to 3mm. Fold the vinyl over the cording. Fold each long end of the vinyl to the inside about ¼″. Pinch the seam with your fingers to get it in place under the presser foot, put the foot down, and then put the needle down to hold it. Adjust your needle position, if necessary, so that you are stitching about ⅛″ from the edge. **A**

**3** Fold each edge of the vinyl inward for a few inches as you sew. Continue to fold and sew until you get about 4″ from the end and then *stop.* Connect the ends of the cording together with masking tape or hot glue and then resume sewing, overlapping the vinyl at the end. Repeat for the other handle. **B & C**

A

B

C

### *Delia's Tip*

This takes patience, and possibly some practice. You may want to get extra cording and vinyl just in case. You might have a few wavy stitches, but overall it gives a really awesome finishing touch and a nice and comfortable strap.

## Assemble the Bag

**1** Fold the darts at each lower corner of the lining and the outer bag pieces, right sides facing, and stitch with a ¼″ seam allowance. Press each seam open. **A**

**2** Pin together the lining pieces with right sides facing, making sure the corner seams match up. Stitch all around the curved edge, leaving a 4″ opening in the bottom for turning. **B**

**3** Repeat for the outer bag pieces and press the seams open for a nice clean look. You should now have an outer bag and a lining.

**4** With the outer bag *wrong side out* and the lining *right side out*, insert the lining into the outer bag with right sides facing. Pin the top edges, matching the notches and corners. Sew around all of the edges. **C**

**5** Clip into each inside corner at a 45° angle and trim each outside corner without cutting through the stitches. **D**

**6** Turn the bag right side out through the lining opening and press. Topstitch around just the side notches. **E**

**7** Fold 1 top seam over the non-overlapped part of a prepared handle and pin evenly. This can take some wiggling and shifting. Just be sure the ends match up at the notches. **F**

**8** Check your sewing machine needle position and adjust as needed so that you are sewing about ⅛″ away from the edge; then sew along the pinned edge. Shift the fabric as you go to keep it flat where you are stitching. Repeat for the second handle. **G**

**9** Adjust the handle in each casing so that the overlap is not seen. Stitch the lining opening closed, and you're done! Good job!

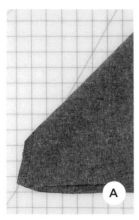

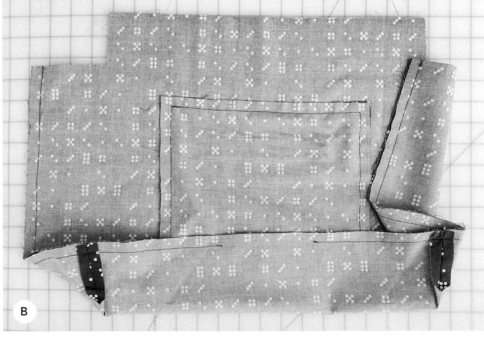

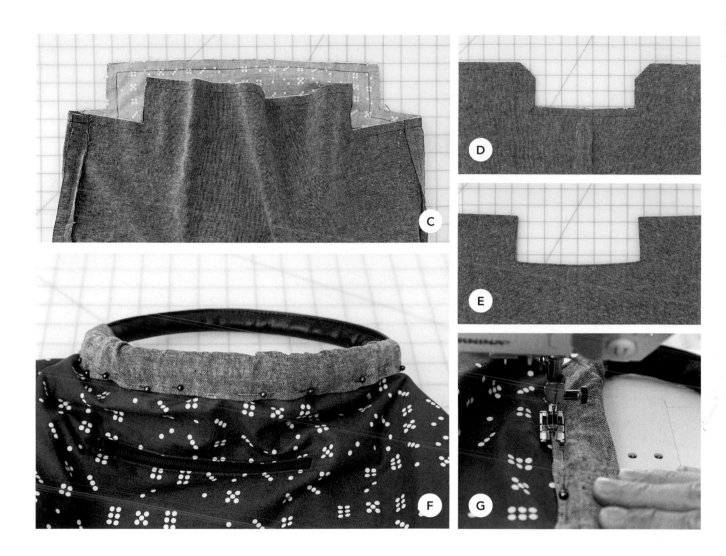

# CHEVRON SHRUG

by Caroline Fairbanks-Critchfield

Chevrons are all the rage, and this little jacket puts them on you! Cute and comfortable, it looks great made with any light- to medium-weight knit fabric that has stripes. A serger is not required for this project.

# MEET THE DESIGNER

Read more about Caroline in About the Authors (page 127).

**Finished size:** varies

**Fabric:** Baby Hacci knit from Girl Charlee

## FABRIC REQUIREMENTS

Fabric must be a 58″–60″-wide striped knit with stripes running perpendicular to the selvage. (If you want to make a cute shrug without the chevron effect, striped fabric is not necessary.) We suggest jersey, interlock, or sweater knit.

Choose the size based on your bust measurement.

| Bust measurement | Women's size | Fabric needed | Collar strip cutting dimensions |
|---|---|---|---|
| 30″–32″ | X-Small | 1 yard | 36.5″ × 6.5″ |
| 33″–34″ | Small | 1¼ yards | 37.5″ × 6.5″ |
| 35″–36″ | Medium | 1¼ yards | 38.5″ × 6.5″ |
| 37″–39″ | Large | 1¼ yards | 39.5″ × 6.5″ |
| 40″–42½″ | X-Large | 1½ yards | 41″ × 6.5″ |

### *Additional supplies*

- **Ballpoint sewing machine needle**
- **Water- or air-soluble fabric-marking pen**
- **Sew-in or fusible stay tape** (sheer tape used to stabilize and prevent stretching)

# CUTTING

✂ *Patterns are on pullout page P4.*

*The key to the chevron design on this shrug is careful layout and cutting. After that, the rest is easy!*

**1** Arrange your fabric on a large cutting area with the fabric folded in half and the selvage edges together. Take care that the stripes are lined up on both the top and bottom of your fabric so the same stripe runs along the bottom layer, up around the fold, and on top of itself on the top layer. This should be the same for the whole piece of fabric.

**2** Place the back pattern piece on the fabric, making sure the diagonal stripe line runs along 1 of the stripes. Place pattern weights over the pattern piece after it is arranged.

**3** Place the front pattern piece on the fabric, ensuring that the diagonal stripe line runs in the direction of the stripes. Move your pattern piece around until the * symbols at the shoulder on the front pattern piece are in the same spot in relation to

the stripes as the * symbols on your back pattern piece. When you are sure that you have arranged your pattern pieces correctly, cut the fabric pieces.

**4** Cut 2 collar strips using the measurements in the Fabric Requirements table (page 13). To create the look on our shrug, cut the collar piece parallel to the selvage.

Fold

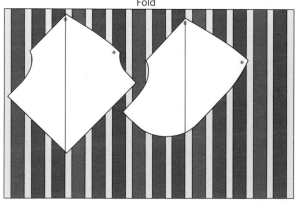

Selvages

# Sewing

*Use a stretch stitch (see Stretch Stitching, page 126) or a serger and ballpoint needle(s).*

*Seam allowances are ½˝ unless otherwise noted.*

**1** Cut 2 pieces of stay tape or seam stabilizer the length of the back shoulder seam. Stitch or fuse it to the wrong side of the back shoulder within the ½˝ seam allowance. **A**

**2** Pin together the back pieces along the center back seam, with right sides facing, matching the stripes; then stitch the seam.

**3** Pin the front pieces to the jacket back at the shoulders, with right sides facing, matching stripes. Stitch the shoulder seams. **B**

**4** Sew a ¼˝ hem on each sleeve edge (see Hemming, page 123).

**5** Stitch the underarm seams, matching the stripes.

**6** Stitch the collar strips together at the short ends, with right sides facing, to form a loop. Fold this in half lengthwise with the wrong sides together. **C**

**7** Pin the collar to the right side of the jacket. Match the seams on the collar to the top and bottom of the seam on the back of the jacket. **D**

**8** Stitch all the way around, stretching the collar slightly. Done! **E**

# HOLLYWOOD SCARF

by Venus Perez

Be glamorous by making this scarf with soft rayon fabrics as we did, or make it in cozy wool to keep you warm all winter. Make sure you pick a lining that you like, because it's totally reversible.

# MEET THE DESIGNER

Growing up in a family of women who sew, Venus Perez has followed in their footsteps. She fondly recalls memories of sitting at the dining table watching her mom sew and listening to her hum a tune. Now a mother of three, Venus sees a lot of her mom in herself. "Nothing gives greater joy and a sense of accomplishment than when my girls wear the outfits I make and tell their friends I made them," says Venus. Crafting is a big part of Venus's life, and sewing is her greatest passion. As a third-generation sewist, Venus hopes her daughters will carry on that gift. Visit Venus at *Suburbia Soup* (suburbia-soup.blogspot.com).

**Finished size:**
70½″ × 13¼″
(not including the hood)

**Fabrics:** Field Study rayon by Anna Maria Horner and Novella rayon by Valori Wells from Free Spirit

## FABRIC REQUIREMENTS

- **For main fabric:** 1½ yards (40″-wide fabric) or 1 yard (54″-wide fabric)

- **For lining and Side Panels 1 and 3:** 1½ yards (40″-wide fabric) or 1 yard (54″-wide fabric)

## CUTTING

✂ *Patterns are on pullout page P3.*

*From main fabric, cut:*

2 using Side Panel 2 pattern piece

1 rectangle 4⅜″ × 18½″ for top panel

2 rectangles 14″ × 36″ for scarf

*From lining fabric, cut:*

2 using Side Panel 1 pattern piece

2 using Side Panel 3 pattern piece

2 using Side Panel Lining pattern piece

1 rectangle 4⅜″ × 18½″ for top lining panel

2 rectangles 14″ × 36″ for scarf lining

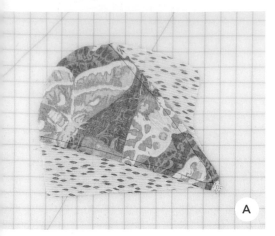

A

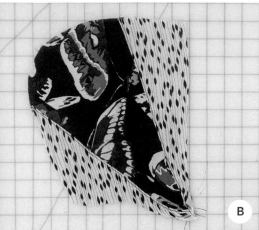

B

# Sewing

*Seam allowances are ⅜″ unless otherwise noted.*

## Make the Outer Hood

**1** With right sides facing and notches matching, stitch side panel 1 to side panel 2 and side panel 2 to side panel 3. Press the seams outward toward side panels 1 and 3. Repeat for the other side of the hood. **A**

**2** Topstitch along the seam on side panels 1 and 3. Repeat for the other side of the hood (see Topstitching, page 126). **B**

**3** With right sides facing, stitch the top panel to a side of the hood, starting from the raw straight edge and easing around the curve. **C**

**4** Repeat for the other side of the hood. Clip along the curves (see Clipping and Notching, page 122). Trim off the excess fabric from the back of the top panel.

**5** Press the seams inward toward the top panel. Topstitch along the seams on the top panel side. Mark the center of the hood top panel in the back. **D**

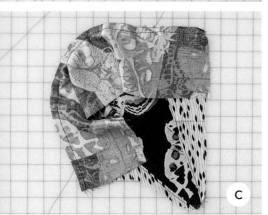

C

D

Mark center.

## Make the Hood Lining

**1** With right sides facing, stitch the side panel lining pieces to the top lining panel. Clip along the curved edges and press the seams inward, toward top lining panel.

**2** Pin outer hood inside hood lining with right sides facing and stitch along the straight raw edge. **A**

**3** Turn the hood right side out, press the seam, and topstitch along the straight edge. **B**

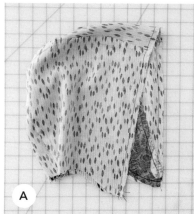

## Make the Scarf

**1** Place the scarf panel rectangles with right sides facing. Stitch along 1 side of the short straight edge to make a 14″ × 71¼″ piece. Repeat for the scarf lining.

**2** With right sides facing, match the center mark on the backside of the hood to the center seam of the scarf. Baste the hood to the scarf ¼″ from the raw edge. **C**

**3** Pin the scarf lining to the scarf with the right sides facing and the hood sandwiched between. **D**

**4** Stitch along the raw edges, leaving a 4″ opening on the side opposite the hood. Trim the corners and turn the hooded scarf right side out.

**5** Press the seams and topstitch ⅛″ from the scarf edge, closing the opening at the same time.

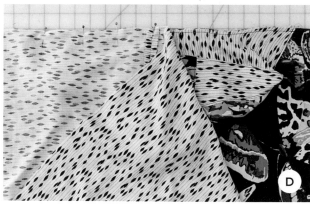

# VENNA TOTE

by Sarah Markos

This lovely cinched tote bag is perfect for travel or a day on the town. It's big enough to carry everything you need and more, with plenty of pockets to keep you organized.

# MEET THE DESIGNER

Read more about Sarah in About the Authors (page 127).

---

**Finished size:** 14½″ tall × 14¾″ wide × 6″ deep

**Fabrics:** Hand Drawn Garden by Anna Maria Horner from Free Spirit

---

## FABRIC REQUIREMENTS

- **For exterior and handles:** 1 yard midweight decorator fabric such as sateen, denim, or twill

- **For lining and flower:** ⅞ yard coordinating cotton

- **For sash and pockets:** ⅝ yard contrasting cotton

- **Fusible fleece:** ¾ yard

- **Midweight fusible interfacing (such as Pellon 931TD or Heat*n*Bond Medium Weight):** 1 yard

### Additional supplies

- **Double-fold bias tape for pocket trim:** 26″

- **Magnetic snap closure**

- **Water- or air-soluble fabric-marking pen**

## CUTTING

### From the exterior fabric, cut:

1 rectangle 22″ × 36″ for the body

2 strips 3½″ × 36″ for the handles

1 strip 3½″ × 9″ for the side loops (This will be subcut to make 2 loops after sewing.)

### From the lining fabric, cut:

1 rectangle 22″ × 36″ for the body

1 strip 3½″ × 40″ for the flower

### From the sash fabric, cut:

1 strip 6″ × 32″ for the sash

2 rectangles 13″ × 16″ for the pockets

### From the fusible fleece, cut:

1 rectangle 22″ × 36″ for the body

2 strips 1¼″ × 36″ for the handles

2 squares 2″ × 2″ for the magnetic snap reinforcement

### From the midweight interfacing, cut:

1 strip 6″ × 32″ for sash interfacing

# Sewing

*Seam allowances are ½″ unless otherwise noted.*

## Prepare the Handles and Side Loops

**1** Fold and press the long edges of a handle strip ½″ toward the wrong side of the fabric. Fold the strip in half lengthwise to match the folded edges and press. Open the folds and insert the interfacing strip into 1 side of the handle. Fold and press again. **A**

**2** Topstitch ⅛″ from each edge of the handle (see Topstitching, page 126).

Repeat for the second handle and the side loop strip. Cut the finished side loop strip in half to form 2 strips 4½″ long. Set them aside. **B**

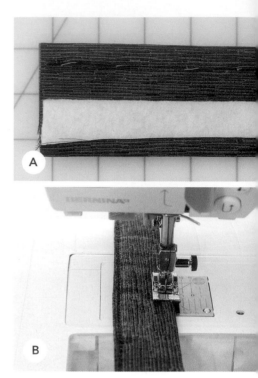

> ### Sarah's Tip
> To prevent the handles from rippling, topstitch each handle starting from the same end.

## Prepare the Pockets

**1** Fold the pocket fabric in half with right sides facing, matching the short ends. Stitch the 2 side seams. Turn the pocket right side out and press it flat.

**2** Slide a strip of bias tape over the raw edge of the pocket, letting it extend about ½″ past the finished pocket sides. Stitch it in place along the edge of the bias tape. Repeat for the second pocket and set the pockets aside. **C**

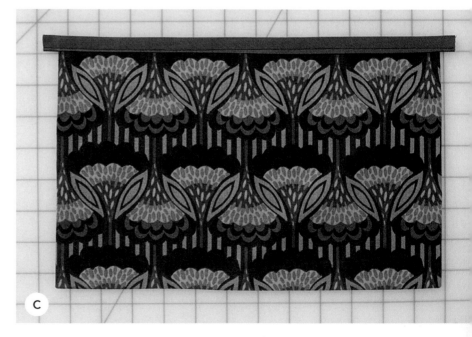

# Prepare the Exterior

**1** Fuse the fleece to the wrong side of the exterior body piece and treat them as 1.

**2** Using a fabric pen, mark the box pleat placement lines on the fleece as shown. **A**

**3** Make a fold along the box pleat line. Stitch the 3″ pleat between the parallel lines 1″ away from the fold. Backstitch securely at each end. Repeat for all 4 box pleats. **B**

**4** Open the folds and flatten evenly on either side of the seamline. Press them firmly with an iron on the front of the fabric.

**5** Attach the handles to the base of each box pleat. Fold under the end ½″, pin, and then topstitch ⅛″ from the folded edge. Sew back and forth 3–4 times. Repeat for the other end of the strap on the neighboring box pleat, making sure the strap is not twisted. The straps will be attached in only 1 place for now. Repeat for the other side. **C**

**6** Fold the exterior body in half with right sides facing and stitch the side seams with a ½″ seam. Press the seams open. **D**

**7** Attach the side loops at each side seam, positioning the base of the loop 6½″ away from the top. The upper end of the loop will be secured during final construction. **E**

**8** Pinch the side seam and bottom together to form a triangle. Pin the triangle to keep the side seam in the center. Draw a line perpendicular to the center seam 3″ away from the corner point. Stitch along the line, backstitching at the beginning and end to create a 6″ gusset. Repeat for the opposite corner and trim away the bulky corners. **F**

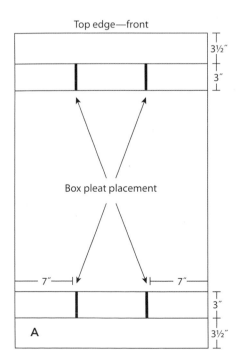

Top edge—front

3½″
3″

Box pleat placement

7″     7″

3″
3½″

**A**

Top edge—back

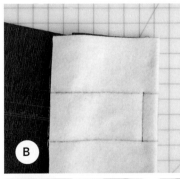

**B**

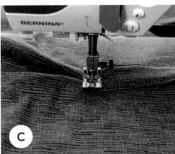

**C**

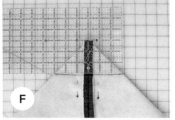

**D**

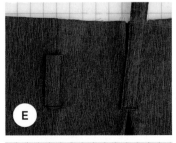

**E**

**F**

# Prepare the Lining

**1** Mark and sew the box pleats on the lining fabric as in Prepare the Exterior, Steps 1–3 (page 23). Press the pleats open.

**2** Place each pocket about 4″ below the top edge. Flare out the fabric below the pleats a little and pin the pocket in place. Some of the fabric will gather under the bottom edge of the pocket. Tuck the bias tape pocket trim under and stitch around the pocket. Sew down the middle of the pocket to create a divider as desired. **A**

**3** Fold the lining in half crosswise with right sides facing, matching the top edges. Sew the sides with a ⅝″ seam. Leave a 4″ opening in the middle of 1 of the side seams for turning. Press the seams open.

**4** Fold the top of the lining in half, matching the side seams, and mark these center folds of each side of the lining with a pin. On each side of the lining, at these center lines, measure 3″ down from the top edge and mark with a marking pen. Center and fuse a small square of fusible fleece to the wrong side of the lining at these points for reinforcement. Insert a half of a magnetic snap at these points, 3″ below the top edge (see Inserting a Magnetic Snap, page 124). **B**

**5** Sew a 6″ gusset in the bottom of the lining, as in Prepare the Exterior, Step 8 (page 23).

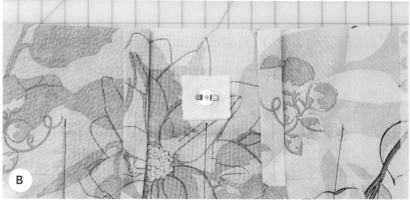

## Assemble the Bag

**1** Slide the lining *inside* the exterior, *right sides facing*. Match the side seams and raw edges and pin. If the openings do not match up nicely, adjust the interior opening by letting out or taking in a side seam. Stitch around the opening with a ⅜″ seam allowance. **C**

**2** Turn the bag right side out by pulling the body through the lining side seam opening. Stitch the opening closed.

**3** Press the top seam flat and topstitch ¼″ away from the top seam.

**4** Finish the handles by topstitching them 3″ away from the previous stitching line. Use a pin to mark the stitch line. Sew through the exterior and the lining of the bag, making sure everything lies flat under the machine. Fold the raw edge of each side loop under ½″ and topstitch 3″ away from previous stitch line. **D**

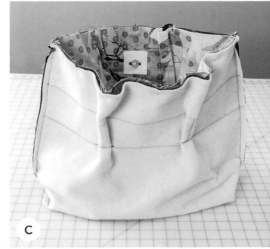

## Make the Sash

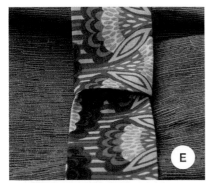

**1** Fuse the interfacing strip to the sash fabric. Fold the sash in half lengthwise with right sides facing. Stitch along the side with a ¼″ seam allowance. Turn the tube right side out and press.

**2** Fold the raw edges of an end to the inside ½″ and press. Thread the sash through the loops and straps, cinching the body of the bag.

**3** Tuck the raw end into the folded end. **E**

**4** Pull out both ends enough to fit them under the sewing machine, and stitch them together. **F**

**5** Even out the sash and position the seam under a side loop.

## Make the Rosette

**1** Fold a short end of the flower strip toward the wrong side ½˝ and press. Fold the strip in half lengthwise with wrong sides together. Trim a curve on the unfolded end. **A**

**2** Starting at the curved corner, sew a gathering stitch ¼˝ from the raw edge. Pull 1 thread to form gathers over the entire length of the strip. Beginning at the curved end, fold the strip over ¼˝ and hand stitch it in place using a needle and thread. **B**

**3** Roll the gathered fabric, hand stitching near the raw edges every ¼˝–½˝. Continue until the rosette is fully formed. **C**

**4** Check to make sure the rosette is securely stitched and hand stitch it onto the sash or a belt loop.

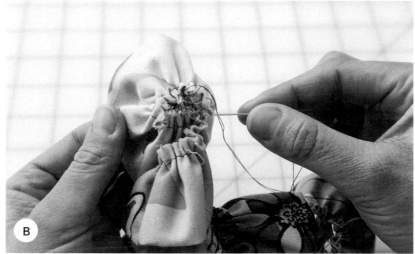

# QUILTING BEE DRESS

by Caroline Fairbanks-Critchfield

This lovely little knee-length dress is your chance to wear your favorite quilting prints! I must admit that I love buying designer quilting cottons, but it's hard to find a pattern casual enough to let me actually wear them. Here's one that's very simple to make and fun to wear.

# MEET THE DESIGNER

Read more about Caroline in About the Authors (page 127).

> **Finished back length:** 39½˝ from nape of neck to hem
>
> **Fabrics:** Cubix by Emily Herrick and Cotton Couture from Michael Miller Fabrics

## FABRIC REQUIREMENTS

This pattern is designed for quilting-weight cotton, but it is also suitable for other light-weight woven fabric including cotton voile or rayon.

Choose the size based on your bust measurement.

| Bust measurement | Women's size | Main fabric | Coordinating fabric |
|---|---|---|---|
| 30˝–32˝ | X-Small | 2⅓ yards | ½ yard |
| 33˝–34˝ | Small | 2½ yards | ½ yard |
| 35˝–36˝ | Medium | 2½ yards | ½ yard |
| 37˝–39˝ | Large | 2½ yards | ½ yard |
| 40˝–42½˝ | X-Large | 2⅝ yards | ½ yard |

### Additional supplies

- **Tear-away embroidery stabilizer:** 1˝ × 1˝ square

- **Water- or air-soluble fabric-marking pen**

- **Bias tape–making tool** (optional)

## CUTTING

*Only one pattern piece is required—it is divided into Part A and Part B on pullout page P3. Trace both parts and tape them together along the line. Transfer the markings for both the front and the back neckline to your pattern piece.*

**NOTE**
To make a tunic version, use only the Part A of the pattern piece. Do not tape the 2 parts together.

## From the main fabric, cut:

**1** To cut out the dress all at once, arrange your fabric in 4 layers, with the 2 folds lined up on top of each other. If your fabric is directional, cut it in half crosswise and turn 1 piece so the direction is the same before stacking the layers. Place the pattern piece along the folds. Cut out using the back neckline marking.

**2** Set 1 cut piece aside—this is the back of the dress.

**3** Recut the neckline of the remaining piece, following the pattern markings for the front neckline. This will be the front.

**4** From the larger fabric scraps, cut 2 strips for the drawstring casing.

BACK

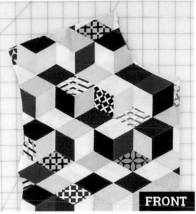

FRONT

Selvages

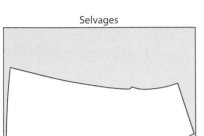

Double fold of fabric

| Dress size | Strip height | Strip length |
|---|---|---|
| XS | 1¾″ | 20″ |
| S | 1¾″ | 21″ |
| M | 1¾″ | 22″ |
| L | 1¾″ | 23″ |
| XL | 1¾″ | 24″ |

### *Caroline's Tip*

I like to cut from the selvage and save the names of my favorite fabrics and designers. These will make the drawstring casing and will not show on the outside.

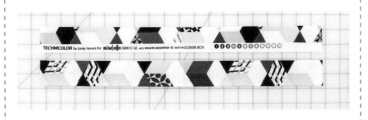

## From the coordinating fabric, cut:

- 2 strips 1¾″ × width of fabric for the drawstring

- 1 square 14″ × 14″ for the bias trim.

  Make 2″-wide continuous double-fold bias trim using this square (see Making Continuous Bias Trim, page 120).

# Sewing

*Seam allowances are ½″ unless otherwise noted.*
*Finish seams with a zigzag stitch or serger.*

## Prepare the Drawstring

**1** Sew together the 2 drawstring strips with right sides facing to make 1 long strip.

**2** Cut the drawstring strip to desired length. Fold and press in the same manner as the bias trim. Fold the short ends in and press. Stitch ends and long side closed.

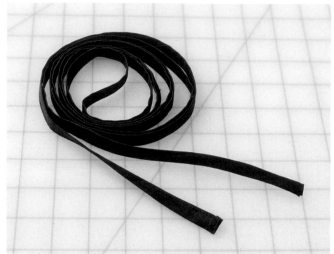

## Prepare the Casing

**1** Place the dress front piece on your work area with the wrong side facing up. Use a ruler and a water- or air-soluble fabric-marking pen to draw a straight line across the dress 4½″ below the armholes. This is the casing placement line. Draw a casing placement line in the same location on the dress back piece. **A**

**2** Measure and draw 2 vertical lines, centered ½″ apart and ½″ long, on the 1″ × 1″ piece of tear-away stabilizer. **B**

**3** Fold the dress front piece in half to find the center. Place the square of stabilizer directly beneath the center of the drawstring placement line (on the wrong side). Sew buttonholes over the 2 vertical lines (see Making Buttonholes, page 123). **C**

**4** Remove the excess stabilizer and cut the buttonholes.

**5** Press all 4 raw edges of the drawstring casing pieces ¼″ to the inside. Stitch the fold down on the short ends only. **D**

**6** On the wrong side of each dress piece, pin a casing piece centered between the sides of the dress with the top of the casing along the placement line. Stitch the top and the bottom of the casings close to the edge. **E**

**7** Pin dress pieces right sides facing and stitch both shoulder seams. Press the seams toward the back. **F**

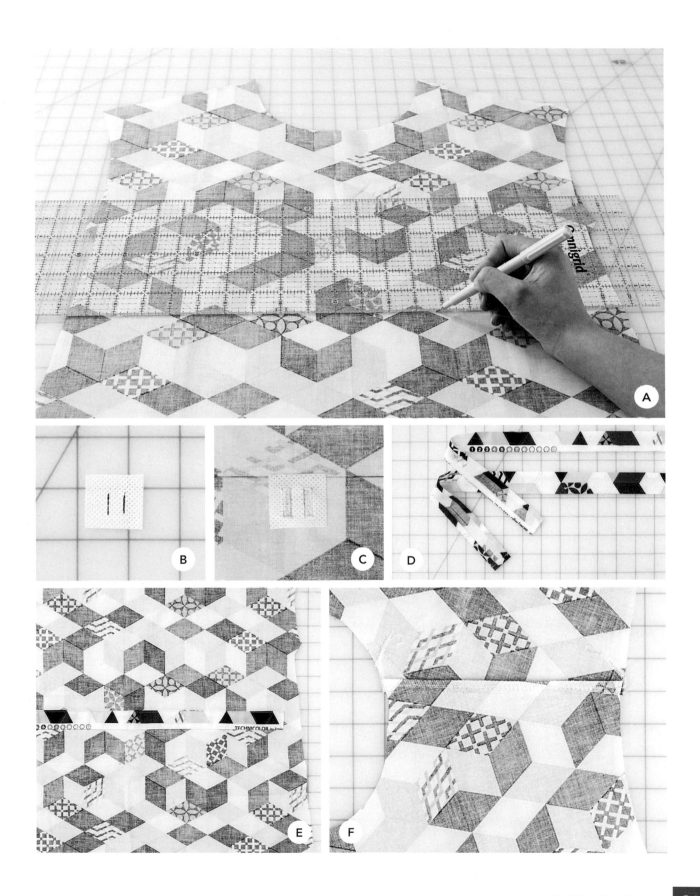

## Apply the Bias Trim Binding

**1** Open a folded side of the bias trim and pin the *right side* of the bias trim to the *wrong side* of the neckline, raw edges lined up. Begin pinning in the center back and leave about 4″ of extra bias trim at both ends. **A**

**2** Begin sewing about 1″ from the center back with a ⅜″ seam allowance, or right in the fold.

**3** Sew around the neckline and stop about 2″ from the starting point, leaving about 2″ without trim. **B**

**4** Finger-press the trim to the neckline until the trim meets, to determine where the seam in the trim should be. Pin together the 2 tails in the center to mark the seam. **C**

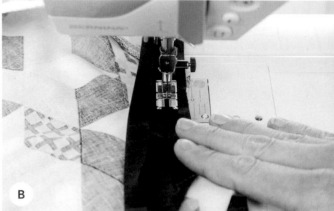

**5** Open the second fold and stitch straight across the 2 tails of bias trim where you placed a pin. **D**

**6** Trim away the extra bias trim to ¼″. Press the seam open. Finish stitching the trim to the remaining 2″ of neckline.

**7** Fold the bias trim to the front around the raw edge of the neckline. Gently press, using steam if necessary, to help the bound neckline lie smoothly. **E**

**8** Pin, if desired, and stitch the binding close to the folded edge from the right side of the dress. Press. **F**

**9** Apply bias trim to the arm openings in the same manner as above, but there is no need to match up the ends. Simply sew the trim to the wrong side of the open armholes, turn and press to the front, and finish with topstitching. **G**

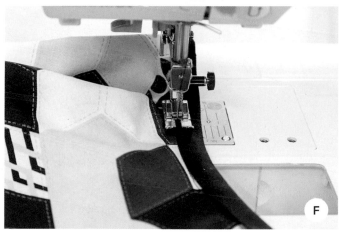

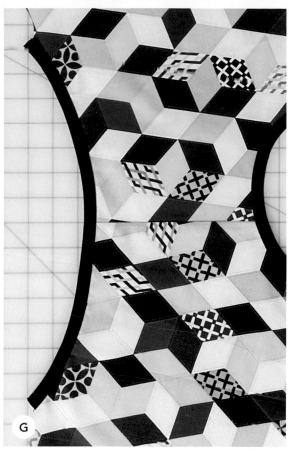

E

F

G

## Assemble the Dress

**1** Pin together the side seams with right sides facing. Stitch from bound edge of the armhole to the hem. Be careful not to catch the drawstring casing in the seam. Clip almost to the stitching in the curve at the top by the armhole (see Clipping and Notching, page 122). **A**

**2** Press and sew a 1″ hem (see Hemming, page 123). **B**

**3** Use a safety pin to thread the drawstring through a buttonhole, around the casings, and out through the other buttonhole. **C**

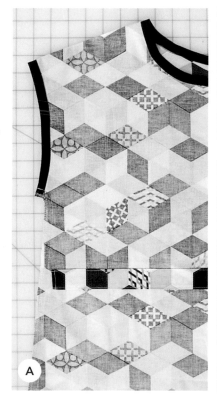

A

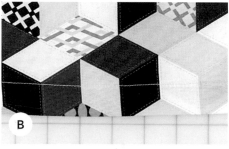

B

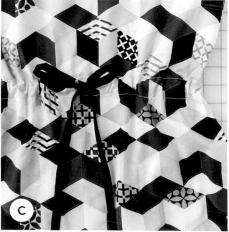

C

# CRAFTY SATCHEL

by Sara Lawson

Create this cute satchel using your favorite fabrics and some chic leather handles. Ample stabilizers give it a professional look.

# MEET THE DESIGNER

Sara Lawson lives with her family in Chicago, Illinois. She has an amazing husband and two wonderful children. Sara loves horses, sewing, photography, books, Australian shepherds, and music. Her blog was named for one of her favorite Jimmy Eat World songs that she had on a cute, pink 7″ record. "It just sounded cool with the word 'sew' in front of it."

Sara started blogging in September 2010 because she loved sewing and was very inspired by the sewing community out in blogland. She is completely intrigued by sewing and loves thinking about sewing pattern instructions, shopping online for fabric, and thinking about new ways to finish projects. Sewing is like solving a puzzle to her—there are always different ways to get from point A to point B, and the fabrics you use and the way you go about making things with them make each sewn item unique. Visit Sara at *Sew Sweetness* (sewsweetness.com).

---

**Finished size:** 14″ wide × 9½″ tall × 3¼″ deep

**Fabrics:** Field Study by Anna Maria Horner from Free Spirit and Carnaby Street by Pat Bravo from Art Gallery Fabrics; handles from BagPurseFrames on Etsy

---

## FABRIC REQUIREMENTS

- **For the exterior:** ½ yard

- **For the lining:** ¾ yard

- **For the flap:** ¼ yard

- **Fusible woven interfacing (such as Shape-Flex):** 1¼ yards

- **Fabric-covered foam batting (such as ByAnnie's Soft and Stable) or fusible interfacing (such as Pellon 971F Thermolam):** ½ yard

## Additional supplies

- **Pair of 28″ leather handles with prepunched tabs**

- **½″ magnetic snap**

- **Water- or air-soluble fabric-marking pen**

- **Hand sewing needles**

- **Heavy thread** (such as tapestry thread, nylon-coated thread, or jeans thread)

- **Quilt binding clips**

## CUTTING

✂ *Patterns are on pullout page P4.*

*All cutting measurements given throughout the pattern are length × width. Please cut your fabric pieces in the order listed so you will have plenty of fabric for the bag.*

### From the exterior fabric, cut:

2 rectangles 15″ × 10¼″ for the exterior main panels

2 exterior side panels using the Side Panel pattern piece

1 rectangle 15″ × 4″ for the exterior bottom panel

### From the lining fabric, cut:

2 rectangles 15″ × 10¼″ for the lining main panels

2 lining side panels using the Side Panel pattern piece

1 rectangle 15″ × 4″ for the lining bottom panel

2 rectangles 9″ × 6″ for the pocket

### From the flap fabric, cut:

2 pieces using the Flap pattern piece for the exterior and lining

### From the fusible woven interfacing, cut:

2 rectangles 15″ × 10¼″ for the lining main panels

2 lining side panels using the Side Panel pattern piece

1 rectangle 15″ × 4″ for the lining bottom panel

1 exterior flap using the Flap pattern piece

### From the fabric-covered foam batting, cut:

2 rectangles 15″ × 10¼″ for the exterior main panels

2 exterior side panels using the Side Panel pattern piece

1 rectangle 15″ × 4″ for the exterior bottom panel

1 lining flap using the Flap pattern piece

# Sewing

*All seam allowances are ½″ unless otherwise noted.*

## Interface the Fabric

**1** Fuse the fusible woven interfacing to the wrong side of the lining bottom panel. Repeat for the lining main panels, lining side panels, and exterior flap.

**2** Baste the fabric-covered foam batting to the wrong side of the exterior bottom panel using a ¼″ seam allowance. Repeat for the exterior main panels, exterior side panels, and lining flap. (See Basting, page 121.)

# Assemble the Lining

**1** Place the 2 pocket pieces together, right sides facing. Sew along the outer edges, leaving a 4″ opening on the top long edge of the pocket. Trim the corners, turn right side out, and press in the opening ½″. Press the entire pocket. **A**

**2** Topstitch ⅛″ from the edge on the side of the pocket with the opening (see Topstitching, page 126).

**3** Pin the pocket to a lining main panel, 2″ above the bottom edge and in the center. The stitched edge of the pocket should be at the top. **B**

**4** Stitch the pocket to the lining main panel using a ⅛″ seam allowance along 3 sides.

**5** Stitch the lining bottom panel to a lining main panel along the 15″ bottom edge. Press the seam toward the bottom panel. **C**

**6** Sew the remaining lining main panel to the other side of the lining bottom panel, leaving a 6″ opening in the center. Press the seam toward the bottom panel.

**7** Place a lining side panel and the sewn lining with right sides facing, matching the top edges. The side panel should be approximately centered across the bottom panel. Pin. Sew the bottom curve first and then the sides, to evenly distribute the fabric. Notch the curved edges (See Clipping and Notching, page 122). Press. Repeat for the remaining lining side panel at the other end of the bag. Leave the lining wrong side out. **D**

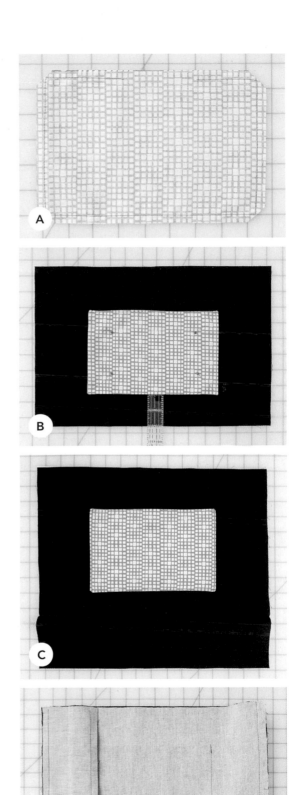

## Assemble and Attach the Flap

**1** Insert the smaller part of the magnetic snap, centered and 1¼" above the cut-out edge of the lining flap (see Inserting a Magnetic Snap, page 124).

**2** Place together the exterior flap and the lining flap with right sides facing. Sew along the side and bottom edges using a ¼" seam allowance, leaving the straight 14" edge unsewn. Clip the curved edges and trim the corners. (See Clipping and Notching, page 122). **A**

**3** Turn the flap right side out and press. Topstitch the finished edge using a ⅛" seam allowance. **B**

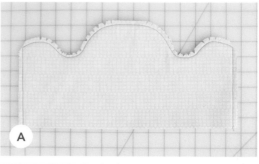

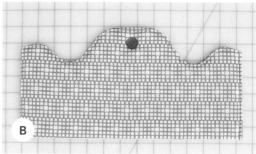

## Assemble the Exterior

**1** Insert the larger half of the magnetic snap, centered about 3¼" down from the top of an exterior main panel. **A**

**2** Repeat Steps 5–7 of Assemble the Lining (page 37) for the respective exterior pieces, except do not leave a 6" opening. Turn the pieces right side out and press.

**3** Place together the flap against the exterior main panel without the snap, with right sides facing. Make sure the raw edges are aligned and the flap is centered. Pin; then baste the flap in place using a ¼" seam allowance. **B**

**4** Temporarily snap the flap to the front of the exterior. Using a leather handle, mark the placement for the leather handle tabs. Make sure that the tabs are free of the flap so that it will be able to open and close freely. Carefully draw an outline of the bottom of each tab to mark placement with a fabric marker. **C**

> ### *Sarah's Tip*
> You can also use the edge of a piece of tape to mark the handle placement without drawing on the fabric.

**5** Measure how many inches down and how many inches between the handle tabs in the previous step. Mark the leather handle tab placement for the back of the exterior to match the front. Remember to factor in the flap seam allowance when measuring the back panel. **D**

**6** Using 2 strong hand-sewing needles and 2 lengths of tapestry or nylon-coated thread, thread each needle and knot the ends. If you don't have access to tapestry thread or nylon thread, double up your regular sewing machine thread.

**7** Place the end of a leather handle just on top of the placement marks and baste the handle in a few places. **E**

**8** Beginning at the top corner of the tab, insert a needle through the right side of the fabric, then the other needle through the wrong side of the fabric, coming out the top hole of the tab. Sew a stitch with each needle, going through the second hole. Stitch back to the first hole to reinforce the beginning and then continue stitching through each hole with each needle. Make sure the tab is taut against the fabric as you sew. Continue bringing each needle up and down through the fabric and the tab, alternating as you go, until you have passed through all the holes in the tab. **F**

**9** When you reach the opposite corner of the handle tab, repeat the stitching through the last 2 holes to reinforce the end; then bring each needle to the wrong side of the fabric. Tie off both ends of the thread securely. **G**

**10** Repeat Steps 6–9 to attach all handle tabs to the bag.

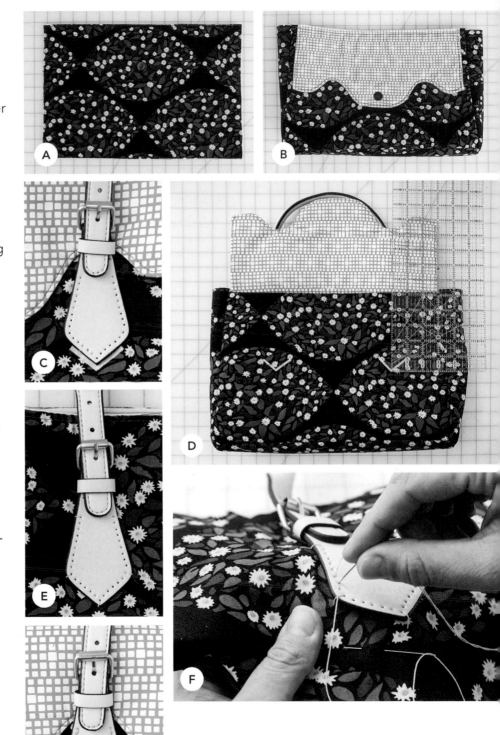

# Finish the Bag

**1** Place the completed lining inside the exterior with right sides facing. The lining side without the pocket goes on the same side as the flap. Make sure that the flap and straps are tucked safely inside. Align the side seams and then pin or clip them in place. Sew along the entire top edge of the bag. **A**

**2** Turn the bag right side out through the hole in the lining. Press. Slipstitch the hole in the lining closed (see Slipstitching, page 126).

**3** Topstitch around the entire top opening ⅛″ from the edge. **B**

# FAUX-WRAP PENCIL SKIRT

by Jen Schumann

This knit skirt has the look of a wrap skirt, giving it that adorable hemline. You will love the comfy yoga waistband. There is no pattern for this skirt—you get to make it to your own measurements and choose the length.

# MEET THE DESIGNER

Jen Schumann is a stay/work-at-home mom of three kids. She grew up with an artist father and a musical, crafty mother and luckily inherited some creative genes, which help her stay sane in a never-ending job.

Fabric is Jen's medium of choice, though very infrequently she dabbles in other types of craft. She loves to design, make, and remake clothes—mainly for her daughter and herself.

When she was fifteen she learned how to sew, a skill that came in handy when formals and prom came around. It was so fun to make her own dress just the way she wanted it, and her date got a matching bow tie and vest (whether he wanted to or not)! She thought her creations looked pretty cool, especially the lacy flowered ones.

Jen started a fashion design program in college but ended up graduating in English instead. After all these years, her fashion designing dreams never went away, and so now in a small way, she is reviving them. Jen's blog is *iCandy handmade* (icandy-handmade.com).

---

**Finished size:** varies

**Fabric:** Black and Creme Stripe Double Knit from Girl Charlee

---

## FABRIC REQUIREMENTS

- **58″–60″-wide knit fabric:** 1–2 yards (at least 30% stretch, not sheer)

> **NOTE**
> You may want to calculate the sizes of your pieces (see Cutting) before you buy your fabric.

### Additional supplies

- **Ballpoint sewing machine needle**
- **Double needle** (ballpoint, if possible)

## CUTTING

*For the skirt panels, cut 2 rectangles of fabric:*

For the width of each rectangle (along the fabric stretch), measure your hips in inches. Multiply this number by 1.5 and subtract 2. Then divide by 2.

For the length of the rectangle, use the desired skirt length measured from waist down plus 1″ for the hem and seam.

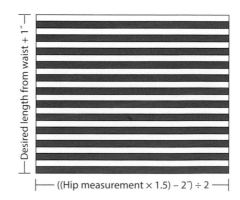

Desired length from waist + 1″

((Hip measurement × 1.5) − 2″) ÷ 2

*For the waistband, cut 1 rectangle of fabric:*

The width of the waistband (along the fabric stretch) is your waist measurement minus 2″–3″, depending on how stretchy your fabric is—for less stretchy fabric, subtract less.

The waistband length is 10″.

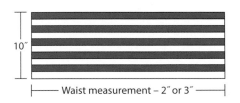

# Sewing

*Seam allowances are ½″ unless otherwise noted.*

*Use a ballpoint needle and stretch stitch (see Stretch Stitching, page 126) or serger.*

**1** With right sides facing, pin together the 2 skirt panels along a side, matching the stripes. Stitch the seam.

**2** Open and press the seam flat.

## Hem the Skirt

**1** Fold the skirt in half along the seam, matching up the stripes across the layers.

**2** Subtract 1″ from your hip measurement and then divide that number by 4. Measure that distance from the seam and mark it with a pin on the bottom of your folded rectangle.

**3** Starting at your pin, cut off the right bottom corner, curving toward the upper right edge of your folded fabric. Try to get a nice even curve. End the curve about 7″ from the top.

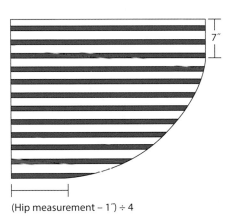

(Hip measurement – 1″) ÷ 4

### Caroline's Tip

Fold your skirt in thirds and check to make sure the curved edges meet in the front of the skirt as you would like them to. Adjust if necessary before moving on.

**4** Starting at the top of a curved side, fold ½″ of fabric toward the wrong side. Press well, using steam if necessary. **A**

**5** Stitch the hem, sewing ½″ from the fold, to catch the raw edge on the underside. Use a double needle so the hem can stretch (see Hemming with a Double Needle, page 124). Press well. **B**

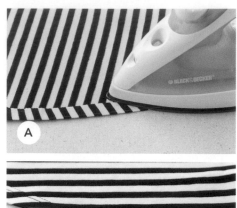

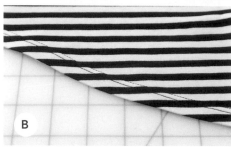

## Fold and Stitch the Skirt

**1** Fold the skirt panel in thirds, overlapping the front panels and lining up the stripes. The seam should be in the middle back. Pin and then baste together the front panels ⅜″ from the top edge (see Basting, page 121). **A**

**2** Pin the right side to the left side along both hemmed edges. Do not catch the skirt back when pinning. **B**

**3** Topstitch along the top curved edge. Stitch right over 1 line of your hem stitch. Go very slowly to be accurate. Do not stitch the back of the skirt to the front. **C**

**4** Using a needle and thread, tack down the bottom curved edge (underneath) in a few spots, including the very top. Make sure your thread is a perfect match so it will not show.

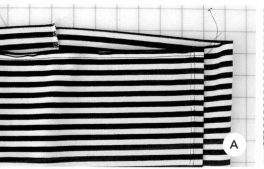

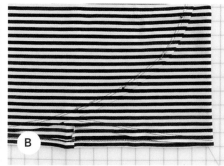

## Make the Waistband

**1** Fold the waistband rectangle in half crosswise with right sides facing. Stitch the short end using a ¼″ seam allowance, making a loop. **D**

**2** Fold the waistband in half, right side out, matching up the seam and placing the raw edges together. **E**

**3** Divide the top of the skirt into quarters and mark with pins. Repeat with the waistband.

**4** Slide the waistband over the skirt with the folded part of the waistband at the bottom and the raw edges at the top. Match up the pins and pin together at each quarter mark. **F**

**5** Stitch the waistband to the skirt, stretching the waistband to fit the skirt. Use a stretch stitch or serger. Press the entire skirt. Done! **G**

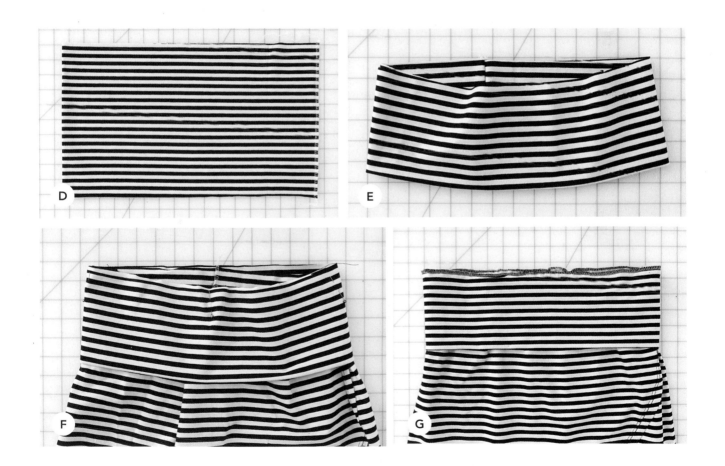

D

E

F

G

# TIED BELT

by Katy Dill

This beautiful statement belt will dress up any plain-Jane outfit. Sew it up in vibrant colors for a pop or in muted tones for a little sophistication.

## MEET THE DESIGNER

Katy married her best friend, Ryan, and is the mother of six baby Dills. The first five are girls, and the exclamation point happened to be a boy! She has always loved anything needle and thread. She also likes to bake and play the harp when she needs something else to do. Coconut, popcorn, and sleeping in are also on her list of favorites. Visit Katy at *no big dill* (nobigdill.com).

---

**Finished size:** varies

**Fabrics:** Faux-Alligator Print vinyl and Clover Sunshine by Allison Glass from Andover Fabrics

---

## FABRIC REQUIREMENTS

- **For belt:** ¼ yard leather, faux leather, or vinyl

- **For ties:** ½ yard lightweight cotton fabric
*Optional:* Use a pretty 3″ ribbon or decorative trim instead of making fabric ties.

### Additional supplies

- **Medium-sized piping:** 2 yards

- **Leather sewing machine needle**

- **Water- or air-soluble fabric-marking pen**

- **Fray Check or similar product** (*optional*)

## CUTTING

*From the vinyl, cut:*

Piece A: (waist measurement minus 2″) × 4″

Piece B: (waist measurement minus 2″) × 2½″

*From the lightweight cotton, cut:*

2 rectangles 6½″ × 27″ for the ties

---

# Sewing

**1** Fold a tie piece in half lengthwise with right sides facing. Draw a curve on an end. Sew along the raw edge with a ¼″ seam allowance and continue along the drawn curve. **A**

**2** Cut off the excess fabric from the corner and clip along the curve (see Clipping and Notching, page 122).

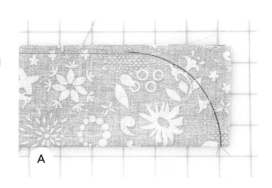

A

**3** Turn the tie right side out through the open end. Use a tool to push out the corner and press flat. Repeat for the other tie. **B**

**4** On vinyl piece A, fold under the 2 long sides ½˝ and stitch about ⅛˝ from the edge. Do not pin, but use binding clips or clothespins to hold in place if needed. **C**

**5** Sew the piping to the long sides of vinyl piece B, aligning the raw edges of the piping with the edge of the vinyl. Use a zipper foot or a piping foot to sew right next to the cord, moving the needle position if necessary. **D**

**6** Fold under the long sides on piece B with the piping along the edge and center it on piece A. Stitch close to the edge of the piping on both sides. **E**

**7** With right sides facing, stitch the ties to each short side of the belt. Trim the seam allowance to ¼˝ and use Fray Check, if needed, or use a zigzag stitch to finish the edge. **F**

**8** Topstitch on the right side of the belt close to the seam (see Topstitching, page 126). **G**

B

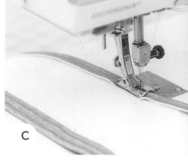

C

### Katy's Tip

If you have a hard time getting the vinyl through the feed dogs, use tissue paper to line each side and then tear it off after stitching.

D

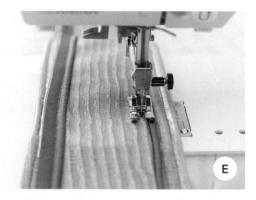

E

F

G

# VERNAZZA COLOR-BLOCKED TOP

by Jessica Kelly

This lovely knit top will quickly become your favorite! It features flattering color-blocked piecing, a comfortable fit, dolman sleeves, and a subtle high-to-low hem.

# MEET THE DESIGNER

Growing up with a mom who made everything from stained-glass windows to wedding gowns, Jessica Kelly learned to appreciate creativity and learning new skills. She sewed a little growing up, but it wasn't until she had her first baby and wanted to save money rather than buy baby clothes that she really dove into sewing. Slowly she became more confident and began creating her own designs for kids and eventually women's clothes. As a taller woman she finds that pants are never long enough, and she can never find long sleeves or jackets that fit, making sewing for herself a solution to orangutan arms! Living in a tiny, isolated desert town with only one stoplight, she also enjoys building furniture, painting, decorating, resurrecting junk into something new, quilting, crafting, and gardening. Creating is a big part of her life, and she has been thrilled to see it rubbing off on her own kids. Visit Jessica at *Running with Scissors* (running-w-scissors.com).

---

**Finished size:** varies

**Fabric:** Navy and off-white rayon/Lycra knit

---

## FABRIC REQUIREMENTS

• 1, 2, or 3 different colors of 60″-wide knit fabric. We recommend cotton/Lycra blend jersey or a similar knit.

Choose your size based on your bust measurement.

**NOTE**

If you sew the center and side pieces in the same color, 1¼ yards will suffice for those panels. You'll still need an extra ½ yard for the upper bodice.

| Bust measurement | Women's size | Fabric needed for upper bodice | Fabric needed for blouse center | Fabric needed for blouse sides |
|---|---|---|---|---|
| 30″–32″ | X-Small | ½ yard | 1 yard | 1 yard |
| 33″–34″ | Small | ½ yard | 1 yard | 1 yard |
| 35″–36″ | Medium | ½ yard | 1 yard | 1 yard |
| 37″–39″ | Large | ½ yard | 1 yard | 1 yard |
| 40″–42½″ | X-Large | ½ yard | 1 yard | 1 yard |

*Additional supplies*

• **Sew-in or fusible stay tape** (sheer tape used to stabilize and prevent stretching)

• **Ballpoint sewing-machine needles**

• **Double needle** (ballpoint if possible)

## CUTTING

✂ *Patterns are on pullout page P2.*

**1** Trace all 6 Vernazza Color-Blocked Top pattern pieces: Upper Bodice Front, Upper Bodice Back, Center Back, Center Front, Side Back, and Side Front.

**2** Cut out each pattern piece in your chosen color. Refer to the pattern pieces for the number of each to cut. Make note of the solid line at waist to lengthen or shorten the torso length.

**3** Cut a binding strip for the neckline 1¾″ × 30″.

# Sewing

*Seam allowances are ½″ unless otherwise noted.*

*Use a ballpoint needle and stretch stitch (see Stretch Stitching, page 126) or serger.*

**1** Cut 2 pieces of stay tape the length of the back shoulder seam. Stitch or fuse the tape to the wrong side of the back shoulder within the ½″ seam allowance. **A**

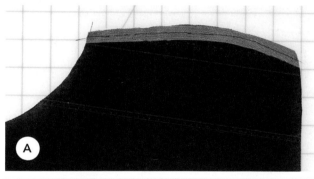

### Caroline's Tip

Premade sew-in or fusible stay tape is inexpensive, but you can also use ½″-wide strips of selvage cut from woven fabric. That's free!

**2** Sew the side sections to the center front and center back. Press the seams toward the side sections. **B**

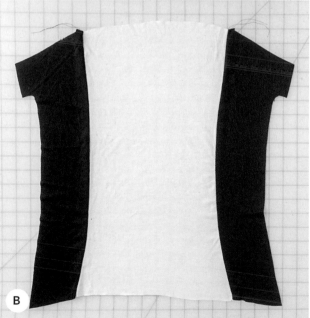

**3** Find the center of the upper bodice front and the front bottom section. Match the center points and side seams. Pin with right sides facing and sew. **C**

**4** Press the seam allowance toward the upper bodice front and topstitch ⅛″ from the seam on the upper bodice front (see Topstitching, page 126). **D**

**5** Repeat Steps 1–3 with the back pieces.

**6** Pin the front to the back with right sides facing and sew the shoulder seams. **E**

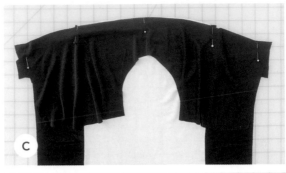

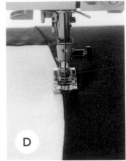

## Sew the Neckline Binding

**1** Pin the right side of the binding strip to the right side of the neckline. Beginning about 1″ from the center back, sew binding to neck with a ⅜″ seam allowance, stopping about 1″ from the center back and leaving about 4″ of extra binding fabric at both ends. This will leave about 2″ of the neckline without trim. **A**

**2** Finger-press the binding to the neckline until the trim meets to determine where the seam in the trim should be. Pin together the ends in the center to mark the seam. **B**

### Caroline's Tip

Stretch the binding strip ever so slightly and evenly as you sew, but don't stretch the blouse as it goes under your machine. This will create smooth, flat binding.

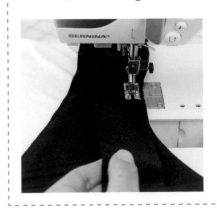

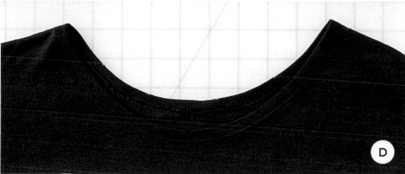

**3** Stitch straight across the 2 ends of the binding where you placed the pin. **C**

**4** Trim away extra binding for a ¼″ seam. Press the seam open. Finish stitching the strip to the remaining 2″ of neckline.

**5** Wrap the binding around to the back of the neckline edge, making it lie flat all the way around. Press and steam if necessary. It is not necessary to fold the raw edge of the binding under. Topstitch the binding from the right side close to the seam. **D**

## Finishing the Top

**1** Open the blouse flat. Press and sew a ¼″ hem on the arm openings (see Hemming, page 123). **E**

**2** Match the side seams with right sides facing and sew the side seams. Be careful to curve around the top of the seam near the armhole area. **F**

**3** Press the hem under ½″. Stitch from the right side using a double needle or a zigzag stitch (see Hemming with a Double Needle, page 124). **G**

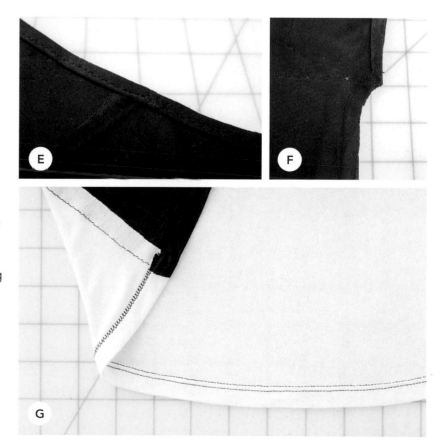

# TRAVEL ETUI

by Ute Barthel

We love to travel abroad, and this little organizer is perfect for our family trips. It is designed to hold everything you need: two to four passports, tickets, vouchers, and printed material. The large compartments will hold a piece of paper folded twice.

# MEET THE DESIGNER

Ute Barthel was born in 1980 in Germany and is the mother of a three-year-old boy. She started to sew in 2003 and was hooked—she decided to attend a private fashion school in Switzerland to get a degree in sewing and pattern making. From there she started her own business selling handmade bags, accessories, and baby blankets. She wanted to get connected with other creative people all over the world, so she started blogging. Her blog is a little bit of everything that makes her happy but focuses mostly on sewing and her creative work. See more of Ute's work at *durbanville.design* (durbanvilledesign.blogspot.com).

---

**Finished size:** *6″ × 9″*

**Fabric:** Modern Meadow by Joel Dewberry from Free Spirit

---

## FABRIC REQUIREMENTS

- **Assorted coordinating cotton fabrics:** ½ yard total

- **Heavy double-sided fusible stiff interfacing** (such as fast2fuse Heavy, Decovil, or Peltex): ¼ yard

- **Small scraps of lightweight fusible interfacing** (such as Pellon 906F)

- **Fusible fleece or batting:** a small scrap

### Additional supplies

- **Sew-in snap, or snap and setter**

## CUTTING

*From the coordinating fabrics, cut:*

    1 rectangle 13″ × 10″ for the exterior

    1 rectangle 11″ × 10″ for the lining

    2 rectangles 7¼″ × 10″ for the document pockets

    1 rectangle 10″ × 10″ for the passport pocket

    2 rectangles 2″ × 3″ for the closure flap

*From the double-sided fusible stiff interfacing, cut:*

    1 rectangle 12″ × 9″ for the exterior interfacing

*From the lightweight fusible interfacing, cut:*

    2 rectangles 2″ × 3″ for the closure flap

*From the fusible fleece or batting, cut:*

    1 rectangle 1½″ × 2½″ for the closure flap padding

# Sewing

*Seam allowances are ⅜″ unless otherwise noted.*

## Prepare the Exterior

**1** Fuse the lightweight interfacing to the wrong sides of the closure flap strips. Fuse the small strip of batting to the center of the interfacing on a side of a closure flap strip. **A**

**2** Pin the 2 closure flap strips with right sides facing. Sew around 3 sides with a ¼″ seam, leaving a short edge open. Trim the corners, turn, and press.

**3** Topstitch around the finished seams of the flap (see Topstitching, page 126). Set aside. **B**

**4** Center the stiff interfacing on the back of the exterior piece and fuse it in place according to manufacturer's instructions.

**5** Center the flap on the front *left* short side of the exterior piece. Pin and sew the flap with a ¼″ seam. **C**

**6** Fold the passport pocket in half, right sides out, and place it over the left side of the exterior on top of the flap, aligning the raw edges. Stitch the side seam. **D**

**7** Attach a side of the snap to the closure flap, centered ¾″ from the end.

**8** Find the center of the opposite short side edge and measure 1½″ in from the edge. Attach the other side of the snap to this point. **E**

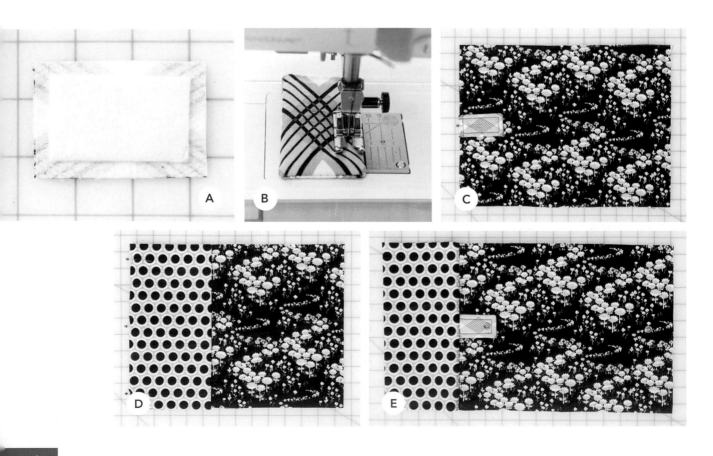

# Prepare the Lining

**1** Fold the document and passport pocket pieces in half lengthwise with right side out and press. Serge or zigzag stitch along the long raw edges. Also serge or zigzag the lining piece along the short sides and serge all around the exterior piece. **A**

**2** Place 1 document pocket onto the right side of the lining piece, aligning the serged/zigzagged edge 1½″ away from the side. Stitch the pocket down along the serged/zigzagged edge. **B**

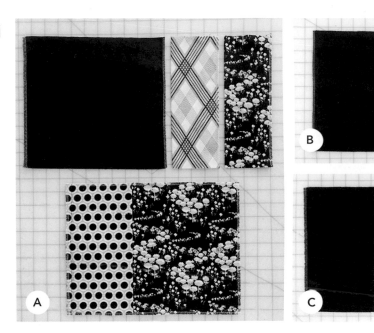

**3** Place the other document pocket on top of the previous pocket and align the edge with the lining piece. Stitch in place just outside the serged/zigzagged edge but within the seam allowance. **C**

# Assemble the Etui

**1** Place the lining piece onto the exterior piece with the right sides facing (the lining piece is shorter than the main piece). Match the passport pocket edge to the end with the document pockets. The other end will stay open for turning. Stitch around the 3 edges, making sure to sew the entire length of each long side. See Ute's Tip (at right).

**2** Trim the corners and turn the exterior right side out through the lining opening. Press well but be careful around the snaps.

**3** Mark the center of the passport compartment and stitch to divide the compartment. Stitch a center line at the fold if desired. **D**

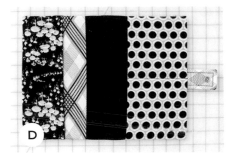

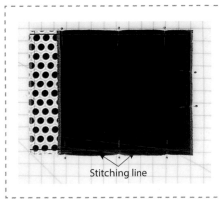

Stitching line

## Ute's Tip

It is better to sew with the exterior piece on top. If you are using heavy interfacing, do not stitch directly onto the interfacing.

# BOHO MAXI DRESS

by Claudia Almandoz

You'll be able to wear this beautiful dress as it is, or jazz it up with a belt. If you tuck in the shoulder straps and wear it at the waist, you have a gorgeous layered boho maxi skirt!

# MEET THE DESIGNER

Claudia has been sewing, designing, creating, writing poetry, and has been behind a camera since the age of thirteen. She studied interior design and art history, and now dedicates her life to her photography: storytelling through images. She is a mother of two and lives with her husband and children in their handmade home surrounded by chickens and a vegetable garden in a small town 38 miles outside Mexico City. She lives every wonderful day on a tireless adventure in search of a simple, sweet, handmade life, collecting images of it all along the way. She blogs at *Mama Bear Says* (mamabearsays.com), and her photography can be seen at Wild Eye Photography (wild-eye.wix.com/foto).

---

**Finished size:** varies

**Fabric:** Black cotton gauze

---

## FABRIC REQUIREMENTS

• Lightweight cotton fabric, including gauze, lawn, or voile. We used black cotton gauze, which was easy to sew and gather.

Choose your size based on your bust measurement.

### Additional supplies

• **Elastic thread**

• **Water- or air-soluble fabric-marking pen**

| Bust measurement | Women's size | Fabric needed |
|---|---|---|
| 30″–32″ | X-Small | 3⅛ yards |
| 33″–34″ | Small | 3⅛ yards |
| 35″–36″ | Medium | 3⅞ yards |
| 37″–39″ | Large | 4⅛ yards |
| 40″–42½″ | X-Large | 4½ yards |

## CUTTING

The body of this beautiful dress is made up of 4 fabric tiers. Based on 44˝-wide fabric, you will need to cut the following strips to make each tier (if your fabric isn't wide enough, piece together strips as needed):

### NOTES

- These measurements are based on 44˝-wide fabric. If you are using wider fabric, you may be able to cut fewer, longer strips.

- If you are 5´4˝ or shorter, you can make this dress petite by making each tier 1˝ shorter.

| Size | Tier 1 | Tier 2 | Tier 3 | Tier 4 | Straps |
|---|---|---|---|---|---|
| X-Small | 1 strip 10˝ × 38˝ | 2 strips 13˝ × 29˝ | 2 strips 13˝ × 43˝ | 3 strips 13˝ × 42˝ | 2 strips 2½˝ × 22˝ |
| Small | 1 strip 10˝ × 40˝ | 2 strips 13˝ × 31˝ | 2 strips 13˝ × 44˝ | 3 strips 13˝ × 44˝ | 2 strips 2½˝ × 22˝ |
| Medium | 1 strip 10˝ × 43˝ | 2 strips 13˝ × 33˝ | 3 strips 13˝ × 33˝ | 4 strips 13˝ × 36˝ | 2 strips 2½˝ × 22˝ |
| Large | 2 strips 10˝ × 24˝ | 2 strips 13˝ × 36˝ | 3 strips 13˝ × 35˝ | 4 strips 13˝ × 40˝ | 2 strips 2½˝ × 22˝ |
| X-Large | 2 strips 10˝ × 26˝ | 2 strips 13˝ × 38˝ | 4 strips 13˝ × 29˝ | 4 strips 13˝ × 43˝ | 2 strips 2½˝ × 22˝ |

# Sewing

Seam allowances are ½˝ unless otherwise noted. Finish seams with a zigzag stitch or serger. White thread is used in most images to show detail.

**1** Sew the strip or set of strips for each tier together at the sides, right sides facing, creating a circle. Mark each circle into quarters at the top and bottom. (You don't need to mark the top of tier 1 or the bottom of tier 4.)

**2** Sew a narrow ¼˝ hem at the top of tier 1 (see Hemming, page 123). This will be the top of the shirred bodice. **A**

**3** Sew gathering stitches at the top of tiers 2, 3, and 4 (see Gathering, page 122).

**4** Place tier 4 inside tier 3, with right sides facing and the top edge of tier 4 lined up with the bottom edge of tier 3. Line up the quarter marks from Step 1 (page 60). Adjust the gathers until the larger tier matches the smaller tier, and pin. Stitch together the tiers. **B**

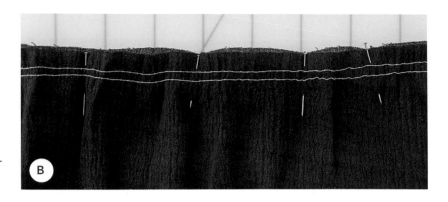

**5** Repeat Step 4 with the remaining tiers, placing the next tier over the tier just sewn, right sides facing. Adjust the gathers and sew. Continue until all the tiers are sewn together and your top strip has a hemmed edge.

## Shirring the Bodice

**1** Hand wind elastic thread in your bobbin with only light tension. Lengthen the stitch on your sewing machine (see Shirring, page 125).

**2** Start shirring at a side seam about ½˝ from the hemmed top. When you reach the end of a row, backstitch over the first few stitches. Then start a new row, 1 presser foot-width away from the last. There is no need to trim threads between rows. **A**

**3** Continue shirring row by row until you've reached the bottom of the tier (about ½˝ from where it joins tier 2). *Note: In this example, the shirring is done with black thread to show proper effect.* **B**

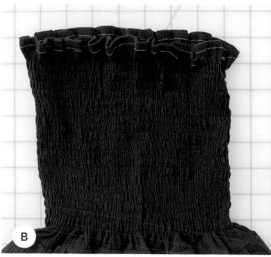

# Finishing

**1** Fold the straps in half with right sides facing. Sew along the length with a ⅜″ seam allowance. Turn right side out using a safety pin. Press the straps flat with the seam on a side. **A**

**2** Pin the end of each shoulder strap at the center back of the dress at a slightly outward angle. **B**

A

## *Claudia's Tip*

You can place the straps wherever you feel they look best. I like placing them almost in the center, right between where your shoulder blades meet.

**3** Stitch each strap to the dress twice, sewing along top shirring lines.

**4** Now slip on your almost-finished dress. Be sure to check that the gathered top fits comfortably. Pull the shoulder straps over your shoulders and pin them in place in the front (this is where you need to check that they are high enough but not pulling too tight). **C**

**5** Carefully take the dress off and sew the straps into place twice.

**6** Hem the dress (see Hemming, page 123).

**7** Iron the hem, sides, and the areas where the different layers of the dress are sewn together. And you are done! D-O-N-E! Yay!

B

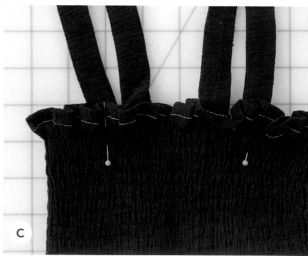

C

# FABRIC-COVERED BEADS NECKLACE WITH CORSAGE

by Sachiko Aldous

Mix your love of fabric with a few jewelry-making supplies to make this beautiful accessory.

# MEET THE DESIGNER

Sachiko Aldous was born and raised in Japan. Growing up, she always loved to draw, sew, and create using whatever she could get her hands on. She kept on creating even more after she moved to the United States in 1995. When the desire struck to share her creations with a broader audience in 2008, she started blogging. On her blog, she shares her sewing and crafting tutorials, some recipes, and a little bit about her life with her family. She has been published in several magazines for her refashioning, sewing, quilt projects, and jewelry making. Visit Sachiko at *Tea Rose Home* (tearosehome.blogspot.com).

---

**Finished size:** 26″ long

**Fabric:** Carnaby Street by Pat Bravo from Art Gallery Fabrics; beads and findings from Fire Mountain Gems and Beads

---

## FABRIC REQUIREMENTS

- **To cover the wooden beads:** ¼ yard of printed fabric

- **For the flowers:** large scraps of solid fabrics

### Additional supplies

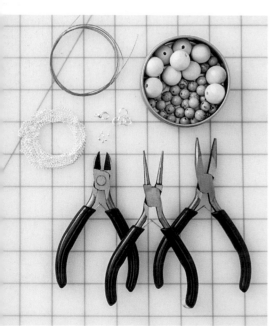

- **Wooden beads:**

    23 pieces if ½″ in diameter

    18 pieces if ¾″ in diameter

    12 pieces if 1″ in diameter

- **Silver chain:** 2 pieces each 18″ long

- **Coordinating glass beads or pearls:** 14″ strand

- **Embroidery thread:** to match your fabric

- **Safety pin or fabric loop turner**

- **Jewelry wire (such as Tiger Tail brand 7-strand beading wire)**

- **1 lobster clasp**

- **2 crimp beads**

- **4 jump rings**

- **Round-nosed jewelry pliers**

- **Wire cutters**

- **For the corsage:**

    **Brooch pin**

    **Fabric glue**

    **Scrap of felt** 1½″ × 2″

## CUTTING

*From the print fabric, cut 1 strip per the bead diameter as listed below:*

For ½″-diameter beads, cut 1 strip 2″ wide × width of fabric.

For ¾″-diameter beads, cut 1 strip 2¾″ wide × width of fabric.

For 1″-diameter beads, cut 1 strip 3½″ wide × width of fabric.

*For the corsage, cut:*

6 squares 2½″ × 2½″ for the small flower

12 squares 3½″ × 3½″ for the large flower

# Make the Necklace

## Make the First Strand

**1** Fold the strips lengthwise in half with right sides facing. Sew along the long edge using a ⅛″ seam allowance. Turn the tube right side out using a safety pin or loop turner. Press. **A**

**2** Slide a bead into the middle of the tube. Insert a needle threaded with embroidery floss through the tube above the bead and wrap it around the tube several times; then tie a knot. **B**

**3** Repeat this process until all the beads are in the tube.

A

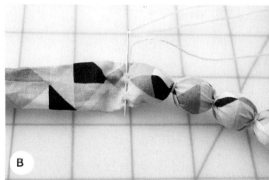
B

C

**4** Fold an 18″-long chain in half and sew the center of the chain to the base of the beads on 1 end. Now you have 1 fabric tube and 2 chains. **C**

**5** Braid the 2 chain sections with the empty tube until you run out of chain. Using your needle and embroidery thread, sew the chain ends to the tube. Wrap embroidery thread around the end of the braid several times and tie it off. **D**

**6** Trim away the extra fabric. Sew a jump ring onto the end. **E**

**7** Repeat Steps 3–4 on the other side of the necklace, except put another jump ring through the end of the lobster clasp and sew it to the other end. **F**

### *Caroline's Tip*

You may choose to either cut your thread between each bead, hiding your knots, or carry the thread along on the inside of the tube.

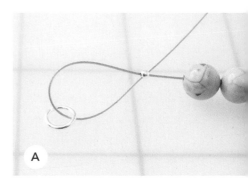

D    E    F

## Make the Second Strand

*The second strand of glass or pearl beads will be 13½″ long. Cut the jewelry wire several inches longer than that.*

**1** On an end of the jewelry wire, place a crimp bead and a jump ring as shown. Flatten the crimp bead with flat-nose pliers, securing it close to the jump ring. **A**

**2** Slide the beads onto the wire.

**3** When you are done stringing all the beads, repeat Step 1 to attach a jump ring to the end. Hide the remaining wire through at least 3 beads. Cut off the excess wire. **B**

**4** Hook the jump ring to the chain at the ends of the fabric-covered beads on the necklace. **C**

A

B

C

# Make the Corsage

*Patterns are on pullout page P2.*

*Use 6 small fabric squares for the small flower and 12 large fabric squares for the large flower (see Cutting, page 65).*

**1** Fold a fabric square into fourths and trace the pattern onto the fabric. Cut out the flower. Repeat for all the squares of the same size. **A**

**2** Pinch the center of the folded petals and sew them together 1 by 1. Sew all the petals together to make a flower. **B, C** & **D**

**3** Repeat Steps 1 and 2 for second flower.

**4** Cut the felt into an oval shape using the Felt Base pattern. Sew the brooch pin to the center of the felt base. Glue both fabric flowers to the felt. **E** & **F**

**5** Add the flower corsage to the necklace to finish it up. Enjoy!

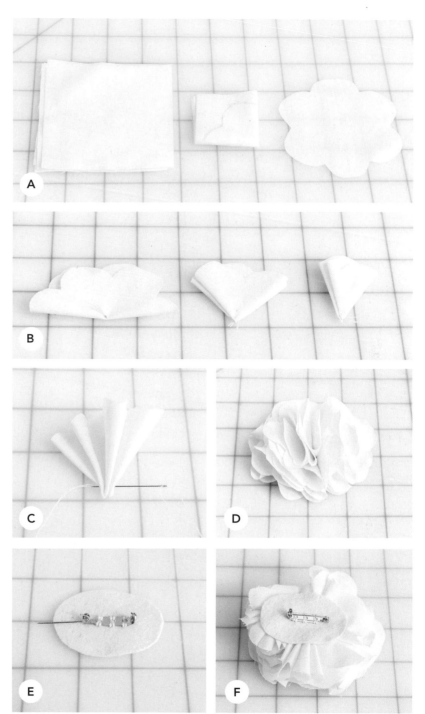

# NIGHT CIRCUS SKIRT

by Kimberlee Turley

This six-gore skirt with a side zipper will bring out your creativity. Sew up a cute black-and-white Night Circus version like ours, or design your own color blocking. You could even go conservative and make all the gores the same color. The waistband fits below the natural waist.

# MEET THE DESIGNER

Kimberlee Turley graduated from the Fashion Institute of Design & Merchandising in San Francisco, California, in 2003. She attributes her passion for sewing to watching Disney's *Sleeping Beauty* daily as a child. In the scene where the fairies make Princess Aurora's birthday dress, Flora cuts a circular hole in the middle of the fabric sheet and says, "That's for the feet to go through." By the age of five, Kimberlee figured out the *correct* way to make a skirt and has been making costumes, clothes, and custom patterns ever since. She casually maintains a blog for her creative sewing and writing endeavors at *Groundwire* (edensguest.blogspot.com).

**Finished skirt length:** 20″ to 22″

**Fabric:** Stretch Vera Sateen from Robert Kaufman

## FABRIC REQUIREMENTS

- **Black bottom-weight fabric (linen, cotton sateen, denim):** ¾ yard
- **White bottom-weight fabric (linen, cotton sateen, denim):** ¾ yard
- **Fusible interfacing (such as medium-weight Heat*n*Bond nonwoven fusible):** 1–1½ yards

*Additional supplies*

- **7″ white invisible zipper**
- **Hook-and-eye closure**

Want to take it to the next level? Consider piecing together the panels and adding hand-stitched accents with embroidery floss for an entirely new look. So many options!

## CUTTING

Use your hip measurement to select your size from the chart. The waistband will fit below the natural waist. Trace the Night Circus Skirt pattern piece from pullout page P1.

*From the black fabric, cut:*

3 pieces using the Night Circus Skirt pattern piece

*From the white fabric, cut:*

3 pieces using the Night Circus Skirt pattern piece

1 waistband strip 3″ × length using the chart. The waistband strip is 2″ longer than necessary to allow for error and will be trimmed to size later.

*From the interfacing, cut:*

1 strip 1½″ tall × length of waistband strip

| Hip measurement | Skirt size | Waistband strip length | Finished skirt waist length |
|---|---|---|---|
| 35½″ | 0 | 34¼″ | 32¼″ |
| 36½″ | 2 | 35″ | 33″ |
| 37½″ | 4 | 36½″ | 34½″ |
| 39″ | 6 | 38″ | 36″ |
| 40½″ | 8 | 39½″ | 37½″ |
| 42″ | 10 | 41″ | 39″ |
| 43½″ | 12 | 42½″ | 40½″* |
| 45″ | 14 | 44″ | 42″* |
| 47″ | 16 | 46″ | 44″* |

*If this is wider than your fabric, cut 2 equal-length pieces and stitch them together to make the required length.*

# Sewing

*All seam allowances are ½″ unless otherwise noted.*

**1** Fold the waistband in half lengthwise, wrong sides together. Press; then open and fuse the interfacing strip to the wrong side of the upper half of the waistband. **A**

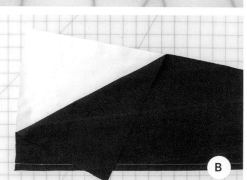

**2** With right sides facing, pin and stitch a black gore piece to a white gore piece along 1 long edge. **B**

**3** Open the skirt panels and pin the next alternating color piece to the raw edge on the right. Stitch. **C**

**4** Continue sewing together black and white pieces in an alternating pattern until all 6 pieces are sewn together. Do not sew the right side seam yet. Finish the seam allowances with a serger or zigzag stitch. Finish both raw edges of the right side (unstitched) seam. Press all seams toward the darker pieces. **D**

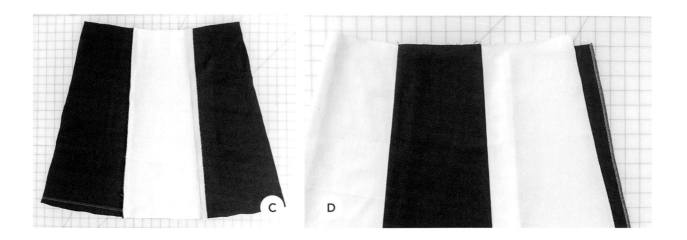

C

D

## Insert the Invisible Zipper

**1** Open the zipper. With right sides facing, pin half of the zipper to the skirt side edge with the zipper teeth over the ½″ seamline. **A**

**2** Stitch close to the zipper teeth using an invisible zipper foot or regular zipper foot. Stop when you can go no further because of the slider. Backstitch. **B**

**3** Close the zipper. Fold the skirt with the front and back sections right sides facing. Pin the other half of the zipper to the opposite skirt edge, right sides facing. **C**

**4** Open the zipper and stitch close to the zipper teeth on the other zipper tape until stopped by the slider. Backstitch. (This time you will use the opposite side of your zipper foot.)

**5** Close the zipper. Pin the front and back skirt sections together below it.

**6** Stitch from the bottom of the zipper to the hem. Try to place your first stitch directly below the zipper stitching. Press the seam open. **D**

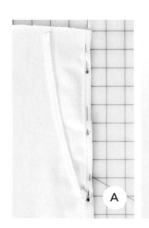

A

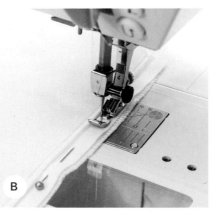

B

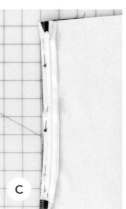

C

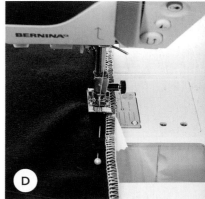

D

## Sew the Waistband

**1** Fold the waistband in half crosswise and mark the center with a pin. Matching the raw edges, pin the top of the waistband (with the interfacing) to the skirt, right sides together, matching the center of the waistband with the left side seam. At the right side of the skirt, the waistband should extend past the zipper teeth about 1″ on the front and the back. **A**

**2** Stitch along the top of the skirt to attach the waistband. Press the seam allowance toward the waistband.

**3** Fold the waistband strip in half, right sides facing, and stitch across each end. Your stitching should follow an imaginary line parallel to the zipper teeth and just past them. **B**

**4** Clip the waistband corners and trim the seam allowance to ⅛″. Turn the waistband right side out.

**5** Press the waistband to form a crisp line along the edge of the interfacing. On the inside, turn the raw edge under ⅜″ and press. Pin the waistband from the outside. Make sure that the turned-under edge covers the line of stitching. **C**

**6** From the right side of the skirt, topstitch the waistband ⅛″ from the seam (see Topstitching, page 126). Check often to ensure that you are catching the folded edge underneath. **D**

**7** Hand sew a hook-and-eye closure to the waistband and tab. **E**

**8** Press and sew a 1″ hem (see Hemming, page 123). **F**

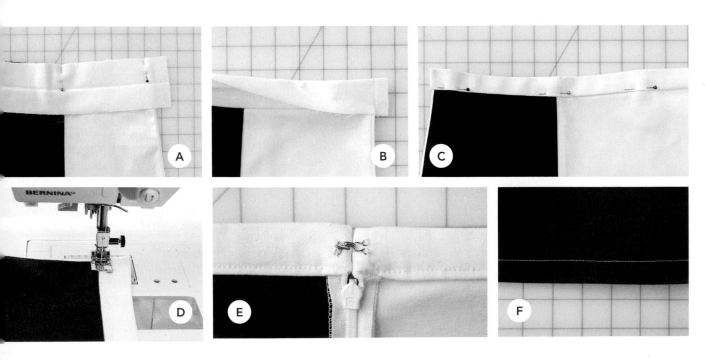

# LACE INFINITY SCARF

by Jessica Christian

Loop this cute scarf around your neck once or twice to keep you warm and stylish! Any type of knit that is 50˝ or wider will work. We used stretch lace fabric for ours.

## MEET THE DESIGNER

Jessica Christian is the sewing maven behind a sewing-centric blog that focuses primarily on children's fashion. Jess's flair for combining vintage fashion with modern-day edge is a breath of fresh air in the sewing world, reaching across all generations of sewists. She also loves to plan parties, bake yummy treats, read when there is time, and be creative whenever she gets the chance! She has an awesome and supportive husband and three little girls—the reasons her sewing obsession started in the first place. Visit Jessica at *Craftiness Is Not Optional* (craftinessisnotoptional.com).

**Finished size:** a loop 50˝–60˝ around and 8˝ wide

**Fabric:** Stretch lace from Fabric.com

## FABRIC REQUIREMENTS

- **50˝ or wider knit fabric (such as jersey, stretch lace, or knit interlock): ½ yard**

*Additional supplies*

- **Ballpoint sewing machine needle**
- **Needle and thread for hand sewing**

## CUTTING

Place the fabric flat on a cutting surface with the selvages aligned. Trim the sides so that they are even.

# Sewing

*Seam allowances are ½˝ unless otherwise noted.*

*Use a ballpoint needle and stretch stitch (see Stretch Stitching, page 126) or serger.*

**1** Fold the fabric in half lengthwise with right sides facing, so that the selvages are at the shorter ends. Sew the long edges together, starting and stopping about 3˝ from each short end.

**2** Turn the fabric tube right side out. You may twist the fabric once or twice before sewing the ends together to make it drape nicely around your neck. Match the right sides together at the seam and sew these short ends together. **A**

**3** Tuck the short seam allowance inside the fabric tube. Use a needle and thread to slipstitch the opening closed. **B**

# SATURDAY NIGHT TUNIC

by Caroline Fairbanks-Critchfield

The only thing easier than wearing this tunic is making it! Throw it on with Ruby's Topstitched Belt (page 81) and some leggings, and your outfit is done.

# MEET THE DESIGNER

Read more about Caroline in About the Authors (page 127).

> **Finished length:** 28½″ from nape of neck to hem
>
> **Fabric:** Soul Blossoms rayon by Amy Butler from Rowan

## FABRIC REQUIREMENTS

- Lightweight woven fabric such as cotton lawn, voile, or rayon

Choose your size based on your bust measurement.

### Additional Supplies

- **Single-fold bias trim:** 2 yards
- **Elastic thread**
- **Clear ruler**
- **Water- or air-soluble fabric-marking pen**

| Bust measurement | Women's size | Fabric needed* |
|---|---|---|
| 30″–32″ | X-Small | 2 yards |
| 33″–34″ | Small | 2 yards |
| 35″–36″ | Medium | 2 yards |
| 37″–39″ | Large | 2 yards |
| 40″–42½″ | X-Large | 2 yards |

*\* Fabric yardage is calculated for 40″-wide fabric. Less fabric may be needed for wider fabric.*

## CUTTING

✂ *Pattern is on pullout page P3.*

**1** Trace Part A of the Tunic pattern piece. Transfer the markings for both the front and the back neckline to your pattern piece.

**2** To cut out the top all at once, arrange your fabric in 4 layers with the 2 folds lined up on top of each other. If your fabric is directional, cut it in half crosswise and turn 1 piece so the direction is the same before stacking the layers. Place the pattern piece along the folds. Cut out 2 pieces at the same time using the back neckline marking.

**NOTE**
To make a cute dress version of this pattern, trace both Part A and Part B and tape them together along the dotted lines. Continue as directed.

Selvages

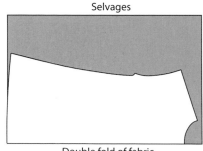

Double fold of fabric

**3** Set aside 1 cut piece—this will be the back.

**4** Recut the neckline of the remaining piece, following the pattern markings for the front neckline. This will be the front.

BACK

FRONT

# Sewing

*Seam allowances are ½″ unless otherwise noted. Finish seams with a zigzag stitch or serger.*

**1** Pin together the front and back pieces with right sides facing and stitch both shoulder seams.

**2** Press the seams toward the back.

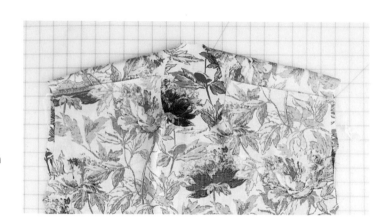

## Apply Bias Trim Facing

**1** Open a folded side of the bias trim and pin it to the right side of the neckline, raw edges lined up. Begin pinning in the center back and leave about 4″ of extra bias trim at both ends. **A**

**2** Begin sewing about 1″ from the center back using a ¼″ seam allowance or sewing right in the fold.

**3** Sew around the neckline and stop about 1″ from the center back, leaving about 2″ without trim. **B**

A

B

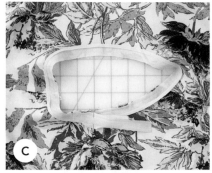

**4** Finger-press the trim to the neckline until the trim meets to determine where the seam in the trim should be. Pin the 2 ends together in the center to mark the seam. **C**

**5** Open the second fold and stitch straight across the 2 ends of the bias trim where you placed the pin. **D**

**6** Trim away the extra bias trim to ¼˝. Press open the seam. Finish stitching the trim to the remaining 2˝ of neckline.

**7** Turn the bias trim all the way to the inside of the neckline. Gently press, using steam if necessary, to help the neckline lie smoothly without the bias trim showing. On the inside, the second raw edge of trim should also be turned under, ready to be stitched down. **E**

**8** Pin the neckline from the right side. Stitch around the neckline from the right side, sewing ⅜˝ from the edge. **F**

**9** Apply bias trim to the arm openings in the same manner as the neckline, except the ends do not need to match up. Simply sew it to the open armholes, turn and press it to the inside, and topstitch. **G**

**10** Pin the side seams with right sides facing. Stitch from the bound edge of the arm-hole to the hem. Clip almost to the stitching in the curve at the top by the armhole (see Clipping and Notching, page 122). **H**

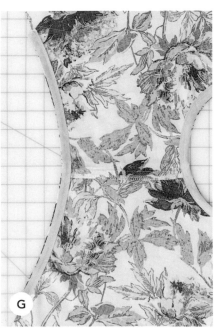

# Finishing

**1** Place the top on your work area right side out. Use a ruler and a fabric pen to draw a straight line across the top, 4½˝ below the armholes. Draw a line on both the front and the back. **A**

**2** Hand wind elastic thread on a bobbin. Lengthen your stitch. Sew a row of shirring over the line you drew. Then sew 3 more rows beneath it placed ¼˝–⅜˝ apart (see Shirring, page 125). **B**

**3** Press and sew a 1˝ hem (see Hemming, page 123).

**A**

**B**

# TOPSTITCHED BELT

by Ruby Bansal

This fun and casual belt is a snap to sew, *and* you get to play with different colors of thread with the topstitching.

# MEET THE DESIGNER

Ruby Bansal's mom taught her how to sew when she was about five, and she pretty much never looked back. When she was growing up, they were always sewing. Whether they were making pajama pants or costumes for a school play, there was always a feeling of "we can make that." Now, much more than when she was a teenager, she appreciates the fact that she can make things for herself and her family.

By day you'll find Ruby working in a university research lab, and at night you'll find her at her sewing machine. The two passions really aren't that different—in both cases, you follow a tried-and-true set of instructions. And when you've truly mastered both skills, you no longer need the instructions and know what shortcuts you can and can't take. Who knew that sewing and science have so much in common? Visit Ruby at *Zaaberry* (zaaberry.blogspot.com).

---

**Finished size:** varies

**Fabric:** Brussels Washer from Robert Kaufman; belt rings from PurseSuppliesRUs

---

## FABRIC REQUIREMENTS

- **Medium-weight fabric (linen, denim, corduroy):** ¼ yard
- **Midweight fusible interfacing (such as fast2fuse MEDIUM or Pellon Craft-Fuse):** ¼ yard

### Additional supplies

- **Topstitch sewing machine needle**
- **Contrasting topstitch thread**
- **2 brass rings:** 1½″ diameter

**NOTE**

Topstitching thread is thicker and stronger than all-purpose thread. The topstitch needle has a larger eye to accommodate it.

## CUTTING

**1** To calculate cutting width, measure the inside diameter of the ring from an inside edge to the other. Add ¼″ to your measurement and then multiply by 4.

### Example:

The inside diameter of my ring was about 1¼″, so 1¼″ + ¼″ = 1½″ × 4 = 6″.

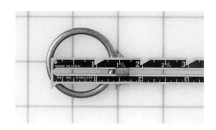

**2** To determine the cutting length, measure around your waist and decide how long you want your belt to be. Add 3″ for seams and folding around rings.

### Example:

My desired length was 34″, so 34″ + 3″ = 37″.

I cut my fabric 6″ × 37″.

*Note: You may have to piece together your belt strip if your desired length of belt is more than your fabric width.*

**3** Cut 1 strip of interfacing, determining the width by using the inside diameter of the ring in Step 1 plus ¼″, and the length by using the cut length of the fabric in Step 2 minus 1½″.

### Example:

The inside diameter of my ring was 1¼″, so 1¼″ + ¼″ = 1½″ wide; and the cut length of the fabric was 37″, so 37″ − 1½″ = 35½″ for length. I cut my interfacing 1½″ × 35½″.

# Preparation

**1** Fold the fabric in half lengthwise and iron. Open up the fabric, fold the sides to the center, and iron. Then refold in half and iron well. **A**

**2** Open up the folded fabric on an end and fold down the short side about ¾″. You need to do this on only 1 end. Place the strip of interfacing inside, matching the end to the folded raw edge. Refold the fabric and press to fuse. **B**

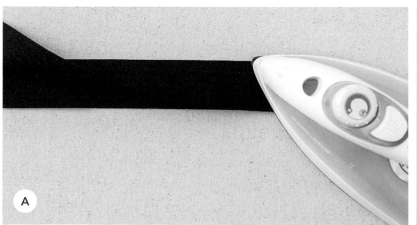

A

B

# Sewing

**1** Insert the topstitching needle in your sewing machine and thread the needle with topstitching thread. Thread the bobbin with regular sewing machine thread.

**2** Increase the stitch length on the machine. Starting at the unfinished end of the belt, topstitch along all 3 finished sides. Then flip the belt over and topstitch in the same manner on the other side of the belt. Try to stitch right on top of the bobbin thread stitch. **A**

**3** Insert the unfinished end through both brass rings and fold it down ½˝ on the unfinished edge. Then fold it over the rings about 1½˝. **B** & **C**

**4** Pin the fold to the belt and secure with 2 lines of parallel stitching. **D**

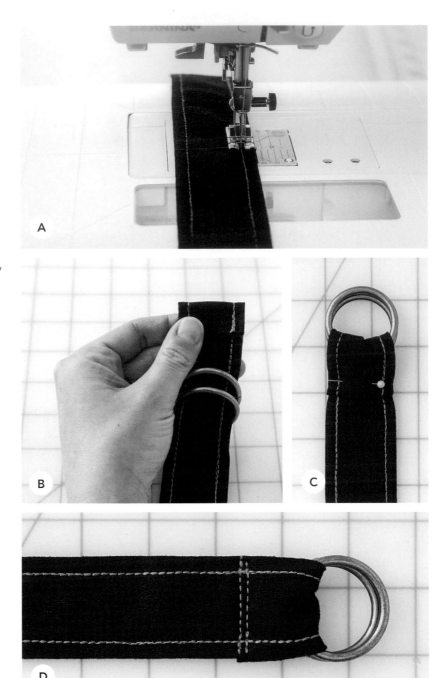

# LOVELY LONG SKIRT

by Bonnie Ferguson

This maxi skirt has six panels that make it fall gently from your hips and flare out at the bottom. With a large fold-over waistband, it is so comfortable that you'll want to wear it whether you go out or stay in.

# MEET THE DESIGNER

Bonnie Ferguson is a busy sewing blogger and pattern designer. She's "Mama" to six amazing children, two girls and four boys, ranging in age from preschool to all grown up. She's also "Gi-Gi" to one beautiful grand-daughter and one handsome grandson. Bonnie is a Jesus follower who is blessed to be married to a wonderful husband who is a huge encourager of her creativeness. (He even cooks dinner regularly, just so she can get her sewing projects finished!)

Bonnie thoroughly enjoys her job designing unique and modern, but always practical, sewing patterns for at-home sewists. She's a self-described "crunchy" mom who wholeheartedly takes on the challenge of reusing and upcycling whenever possible. In addition to sewing, she loves coffee, home-schooling, dark chocolate, worship music, babies, all things vintage, home decorating, cooking, and science fiction. See what she is up to at *Fishsticks Designs* (fishsticksdesigns.com).

---

**Finished length (from waistband seam):** 39″

**Fabric:** Grass Laguna cotton jersey from Robert Kaufman

---

## FABRIC REQUIREMENTS

*For the panels and the waistband*

**Cotton/spandex or 58″-wide cotton/Lycra jersey fabric:** 3 yards (3½ yards if the fabric is directional)

*OR*

*For the panels*

**Cotton or 58″-wide cotton blend jersey:** 2½ yards (3 yards if the fabric is directional)

*For the waistband*

**58″-wide cotton/spandex or 58″-wide cotton/Lycra jersey:** ½ yard

---

### Bonnie's Tip: Choosing the right fabric

Cotton or cotton blend jerseys are recommended for the best results in the panels. Cotton or cotton blend interlocks will work as well but will not curl at the hem.

Cotton/spandex or cotton/Lycra jersey or rib knit is recommended for the waistband. Cotton knits without spandex or Lycra will not have the recovery to work properly in the waistband.

*Additional supplies (optional)*

- **Stretchy nylon bobbin thread (such as Woolly Nylon):** to give your stitches a little extra stretch

- **Walking foot:** to help to prevent waviness in your finished seams

## CUTTING

✂ *Pattern is on pullout page P1.*

*From the main fabric, cut:*

6 panels using the Upper and Lower Skirt Panel pattern piece

### NOTE

The Upper Skirt Panel and Lower Skirt Panel patterns must be joined before cutting the fabric.

*From the waistband fabric, cut:*

1 rectangle using the following chart

| Waist measurement | Hip measurement | Skirt size | Waistband strip width | Waistband strip length (direction of most stretch) |
|---|---|---|---|---|
| 24″–25″ | 35½″–37″ | XS (0–2) | 17″ | 25″ |
| 26″–28″ | 37½″– 40″ | S (4–6) | 17″ | 28″ |
| 29″–31″ | 40½″–43″ | M (8–10) | 17″ | 31″ |
| 32″–35″ | 43½″–47″ | L (12–14) | 17″ | 35″ |
| 36″–39″ | 47½″–50″ | XL (16–18) | 17″ | 39″ |

# Sewing

*Seam allowances are ½″ unless otherwise noted.*

**1** Begin assembling the panels by placing together 2 with right sides facing. Pin along a curved edge and stitch from the waist to the hem to keep the pointed edge from getting caught under the foot of your sewing machine. **A**

**2** Add a third panel to make the front. **B**

**3** Sew together the remaining 3 panels of the skirt to form the back of the skirt.

**4** Place together the front and back of the skirt with the right sides facing. Pin and stitch together the skirt on each side. Press all the seams open. **C**

### Bonnie's Tip

For the best results, sew together the panels with the stretch stitch on your sewing machine rather than serging them together (see Stretch Stitching, page 126). Because the seam allowance will show a bit at the curled edges of the hem, this makes for a nicer finished look. The waistband can be sewn or serged.

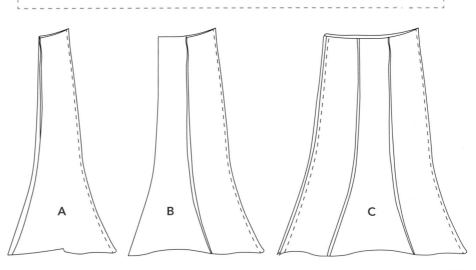

## Sew the Waistband

**1** Fold the waistband in half crosswise, as shown, right sides facing. Pin together the short edges. Sew or serge across the pinned edge. **A**

**2** Mark the center front point and both of the side points on the waistband with a marking pen or pin. Mark the center of both the front and the back center panels on the skirt. **B**

**3** Fold the waistband in half lengthwise with wrong sides together, lining up the long raw edges. **C**

**4** With the skirt inside out, slide the waistband inside the skirt, matching the waistband seam with the back center of the skirt. Match the front and side marks on the waistband to the center front and side seams of the skirt. Pin in place using 2 pins at each side seam to pin the seam allowances on the skirt open. Stretch the waistband flat against the skirt between each set of pins to find where to pin the remaining seams. Pin the

waistband to the skirt at each of these points, pinning all the seams open. **D**

**5** Sew or serge all the way around the waist, stretching the waistband slightly and evenly as you go. **E**

**6** Flip the waistband up and your sewing is done! **F**

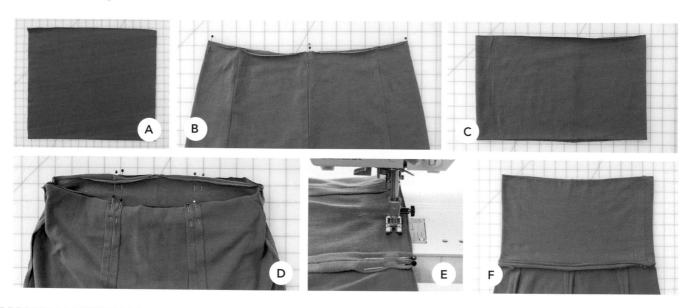

## Finishing

Turn the skirt right side out and trim away any uneven edges along the bottom of the skirt. To get the curled effect on the raw-edge hem,

you'll just need to wash and dry the skirt and it will be ready to wear!

Alternate finished hem: Press the hem ½˝ to the wrong side.

Stitch on the right side using a double needle (see Hemming with a Double Needle, page 124).

# PAINTER'S CLUTCH

by Sarah Markos

This little clutch has the classic look of a fold-over with the convenience of handles when you need them. It gets its name from the paint-stirring sticks that are used for the handles. You probably have a couple of them lying around just waiting to be used.

# MEET THE DESIGNER

Read more about Sarah in About the Authors (page 127).

**Finished size:** 12″ × 11½″

**Fabric:** Hand Drawn Garden by Anna Maria Horner from Free Spirit

## FABRIC REQUIREMENTS

- **For exterior:** ½ yard quilting cotton

- **For lining and divider pocket:** ¾ yard quilting cotton

- **Fusible heavyweight interfacing (such as Pellon 808 Craft-Fuse):** ½ yard

- **13″ double-fold bias trim or twill tape**

### Additional supplies

- **Invisible sew-in magnetic snap**

- **For handles:** 2 paint-stirring sticks or ½″ wooden dowels

- **Spray paint or craft paint:** in a coordinating color for the handles

- **Sturdy craft scissors or saw**

- **Turning tool**

## CUTTING

✂ *Pattern is on pullout page P3.*

### From the exterior fabric, cut:

2 pieces on the fold using the Painter's Clutch pattern

### From the lining fabric, cut:

2 pieces on the fold using the Painter's Clutch pattern

1 square 14″ × 14″ for the divider pocket

### From the heavyweight interfacing, cut:

2 pieces on the fold using the Painter's Clutch pattern

# Preparation

**1** Transfer the magnetic snap placement marking onto the nonfusible side of the interfacing pieces.

**2** Fuse the interfacing to the wrong side of the lining pieces.

**3** Cut the paint sticks or dowel rod into 2 handles

8½″ long using sturdy craft scissors or a saw.

**4** Paint the handles and set them aside to dry.

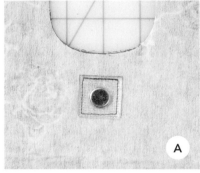

# Sewing

*Seam allowances are ¼″ unless otherwise noted.*

**1** Place the flat side of a sew-in magnetic snap on the wrong side of a lining piece at the marking. Sew around the plastic edges of the snap. Sew the other side of the snap to the other lining piece. Check to make sure the magnets attract correctly. **A**

**2** Place an exterior piece on top of a lining piece with right sides facing and pin. Stitch around the upper part of the clutch. **B**

**3** Using sharp, pointed scissors, trim the corners and clip the curves (see Clipping and Notching, page 122).

**4** Turn the piece right side out using a tool to push out the corners. Press all the seams flat.

**5** Repeat Steps 1–4 for the other half of the clutch.

**6** Make a casing for the handle by folding the top seam to the front 1¾″ and pinning. Check to make sure this casing will be wide enough for the handle to slide through easily. Adjust if necessary. Topstitch along the bottom of the casing, backstitching at the beginning and end. Repeat for all 4 corners. **C**

## Sarah's Tip

For an alternative look, you can fold the top seam to the back and you won't see the lining fabric.

**7** Fold the pocket fabric in half and topstitch along the folded edge.

**8** Place a side of the clutch on the table with the lining facing up. Place the pocket on top of it, matching the bottom edges. Place the other side of the clutch on top with the lining side down. Pin the sides. Stitch the side seams, backstitching at the top. **D**

**9** Trim the seam allowance to ⅛″.

**10** Turn the clutch *lining side out* and press the seams flat. Stitch the side seams again.

Begin sewing from the bottom corner and backstitch 3–4 times at the top. This second line of stitching will enclose the raw edge and is called a French seam. **E**

**11** Stitch the bottom seam. Trim the seam allowance, if necessary, to make it even and trim the corners.

**12** Fold the bias tape around the raw edge of the bottom seam and topstitch. Trim the tape so it is flush with

the clipped corner, leaving the end unfinished. Turn the clutch right side out and press flat. **F**

**13** Sew a few stitches on an end of the casing. Thread the handle through both casings, pushing it all the way to the sewn end. Slide the handle away from the other end so that it will not be in the way of the machine. Sew a few stitches on this end to prevent the handle from sliding out. Repeat for the other handle. **G**

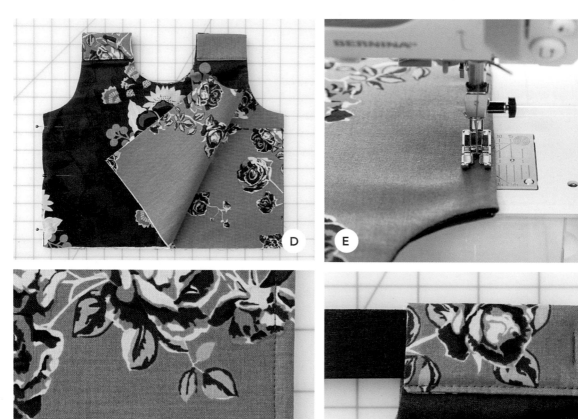

# PRETTY POCKETS APRON

by Maureen Cracknell

With only five fat quarters you can create this super-cute apron. My favorite part is that the bottom skirt fabric stays draped, so you can lift the linen side panels to wipe your hands—almost like hanging tea towels! Love that! Plus, the wide waistband makes this apron easy to wear and flattering for all shapes. The angled side panel pieces add a sweet femininity and flirtiness, too!

# MEET THE DESIGNER

 Maureen is a busy mother of three who loves all things crafty and creative. She makes things by hand at home in a small town in Pennsylvania. She started blogging in 2010 to have a little space of her own to share her passion and to create and document what she learns and how she grows as an artistic person. It is her special place to keep and share all of her projects and the projects that she and her children create *together*.

Maureen is a Riley Blake Design Team member, an independent designer for Janome, a part of the Art Gallery Fabrics Fat Quarter Gang, and a new addition to the Therm O Web Design Team! She is incredibly thankful to be a part of the online sewing community and feels blessed to be able to make and seek out new artistic goals because of the support and encouragement she receives. See what Maureen creates at *Maureen Cracknell Handmade* (maureencracknellhandmade.blogspot.com).

---

**Finished size:** 21˝ × 20¼˝

**Fabrics:** Splendor 1920 by Bari J. and Luxe in Bloom by Sarah Watson from Art Gallery Fabrics

---

## FABRIC REQUIREMENTS

*A fat quarter is a piece of fabric that measures 18˝ × 22˝.*

- **For the main apron fabric:** 1 fat quarter
- **For the side panel fabrics:** 1 fat quarter of cotton linen
- **For apron pockets:** 1 fat quarter of cotton linen
- **For the waistband:** 1 fat quarter
- **For the ties:** 1 fat quarter
- **For the appliqué:** a variety of coordinating fabric scraps

### Additional supplies

- **Iron-on fusible web such as HeatnBond Lite or Pellon Wonder-Under**

## CUTTING

*From the 5 fat quarters, cut:*

- 1 rectangle 18˝ × 22˝ for the main apron fabric
- 2 rectangles 11˝ × 18˝ for the side panel fabrics
- 2 rectangles 11˝ × 12˝ for each pocket
- 1 rectangle 9˝ × 22˝ for the waistband
- 2 rectangles 7˝ × 22˝ for the ties

# Sewing

## Create the Apron Skirt

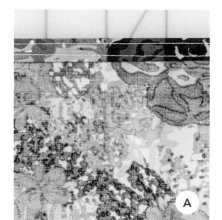

**1** Press and pin a ¼″ hem at the bottom (22″) and side (18″) edges of the main apron rectangle (see Hemming, page 123).

**2** Sew along the inner folded edge and the outer edge to create a double-stitched seam on the bottom and 2 sides. **A**

**3** As described in Steps 1 and 2, hem the bottom and each side of the linen panel pieces. There is no need to hem the top. **B**

**4** To create the pockets, sew a single-stitched hem on the bottom and sides of both linen pocket pieces, this time sewing just along the inner edge of the fold. Sew a double-stitched hem at the top edge of the pocket pieces. **C**

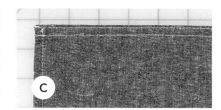

## Add the Pocket Appliqué

*Patterns are on pullout page P3.*

**1** Trace the appliqué shapes onto the paper backing of the iron-on fusible web. Cut out the shapes ⅛″ outside the drawn line. Following the manufacturer's instructions, fuse these shapes onto the wrong side of each fabric scrap. **D**

**2** Cut out the shapes on the drawn line. Remove the paper backing from each shape and position it on the linen pocket, arranging them as shown on the finished apron or as desired. Fuse the shapes to the linen using a hot iron.

**3** Using a thread that matches or coordinates with each fabric shape, sew the shapes to the linen using a zigzag or appliqué stitch.

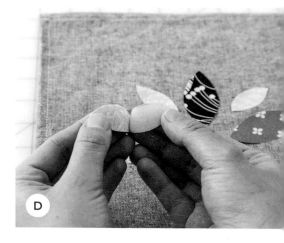

## Attach the Pockets

**1** Place each pocket 2½″ above the bottom edge of each apron side panel, matching the side edges. Pin them in place. **A**

**2** Topstitch the pockets onto the apron by sewing along the outer edge along the sides and bottom of the pocket, leaving the top of the pocket open.

**3** Place each pocket panel piece on top of the hemmed skirt piece at a slight angle as shown. After the panel pieces are positioned, pin or baste them in place and set them aside. **B**

## Create the Waistband and Ties

**1** Fold under ¼″ on each edge of the waistband and press. Fold this piece in half so the sides match up and press well. The pressed waistband should have no exposed raw edges. **C**

**2** Place the finished apron skirt inside the waistband so that the waistband covers the raw edges at the top of the apron skirt and the pocket panels. Check that both sides are even and pin in place. **D**

**3** Sew along both the top and the bottom of the waistband, staying close to the edge, leaving both sides of the waistband open for the ties.

**4** Fold under ¼″ on both long and 1 short tie edge of each tie piece. Press, fold them in half lengthwise, and press again. **E**

**5** Sew along the outside edge of each tie, staying close to the edge.

**6** Insert the tie into the opening on each side of the waistband and pin it in place. **F**

**7** Sew the ties in place with 2 rows of stitching. **G**

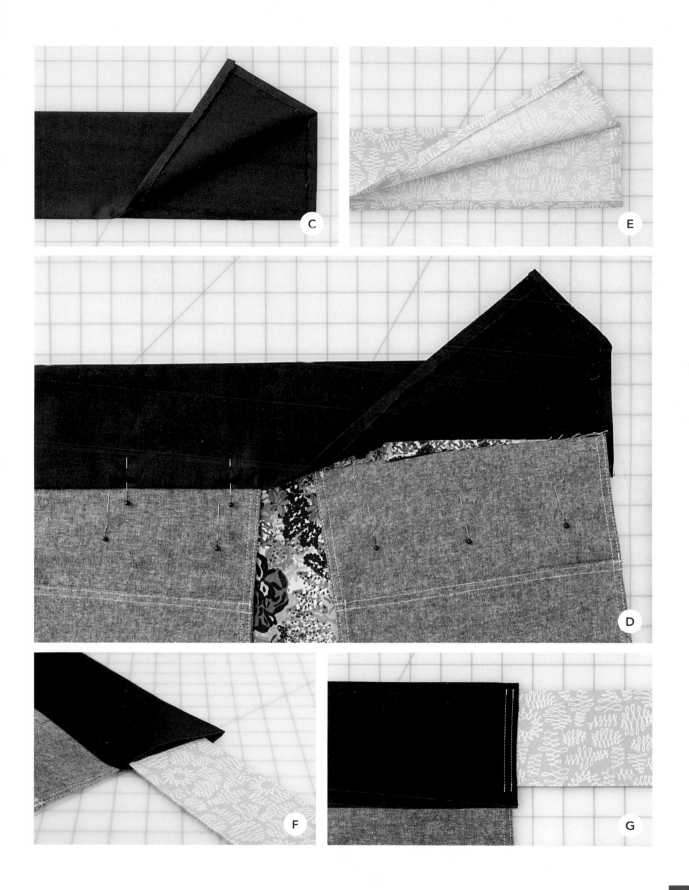

# RETRO URBAN APRON

by Leslie Rutland

This fun and flirty apron will keep you covered while whipping up your favorite holiday meals.

# MEET THE DESIGNER

Leslie Rutland is the founder and designer of Sugar Pie Chic Patterns. With her blog, she is spreading the word that anyone can sew. She blogs with the beginner in mind, sharing sewing tips, tutorials, and patterns. She works from her sunny studio in Austin, Texas, and draws much of her inspiration from the Texas Hill Country. When she's not hoarding fabric, Leslie loves to read to her grandchildren, grow vegetables, and make really great gluten-free food. Visit Leslie at *The Seasoned Homemaker* (seasonedhomemaker.com).

**Finished size:** 33″ wide at the hips and 29″ long

**Fabric:** Moxie by Erin McMorris from Free Spirit

## FABRIC REQUIREMENTS

- **For the apron skirt:** 1 yard cotton
- **Cotton in a coordinating print:** ¾ yard
- **Cotton in a contrasting print or solid:** ⅜ yard

### Additional supplies

- **Water- or air-soluble fabric-marking pen**

## CUTTING

### From the apron skirt fabric, cut:

1 rectangle 34″ × 17″ for the apron skirt

1 rectangle 4″ × 6″ for the pocket

1 rectangle 3″ × 6″ for the pocket trim

### From the coordinating fabric, cut:

1 rectangle 11″ × 22″ for the apron bodice

2 strips 4″ × 30″ for the waist ties

2 strips 2¾″ × 35″ for the ruffled hem band

1 strip 2″ × 12″ for the gathered pocket band

### From the contrasting fabric, cut:

1 strip 2″ × 40″ for the neck tie

2 strips 2¾″ × 28″ for the waistband and lining

2 strips 1½″ × 35″ for the hem band trim

# Sewing

*Seam allowances are ½″ unless otherwise noted.*

## Prepare the Pocket

**1** Sew gathering stitches along the top and bottom edges of the gathered pocket band within the ⅜″ seam allowance. Adjust the gathers until the gathered pocket band is 6″ wide (see Gathering, page 122).

**2** With wrong sides together, fold the pocket trim in half lengthwise. Press.

**3** With right sides facing, pin the pocket trim to the gathered pocket band. Stitch together the pieces with a ⅜″ seam. **A**

**4** Press the seam allowance up and topstitch close to the seam. With right sides facing, pin the larger pocket piece to the bottom edge of the gathered pocket band. Stitch the pieces together with a ⅜″ seam. Press the seam allowance down. Topstitch close to the seam. **B**

**5** Fold the side and bottom edges of the pocket under ¼″ and press. Pin the pocket to the apron skirt piece with the top edge of the pocket 6″ from the top edge of the apron skirt and the left edge of the pocket 9″ from the left edge of the apron skirt. **C**

**6** Stitch around the sides and bottom of the pocket ⅛″ from the edge.

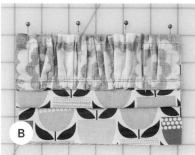

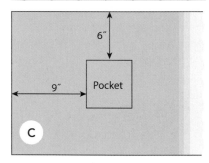

## Prepare the Ruffled Hem Band

**1** Pin and stitch the 2 ruffled hem band strips together with a ⅜″ seam. Press the seam open. Set aside.

**2** Pin and stitch the 2 hem band trim strips together with a ⅜″ seam. Press the seam open. Fold the hem band trim piece in half lengthwise, wrong sides together, and press.

**3** With right sides facing and raw edges matching, pin the hem band trim fabric to the ruffled hem band. Stitch together the pieces using a ¼″ seam. Finish the seams with a zigzag stitch or serger as desired.

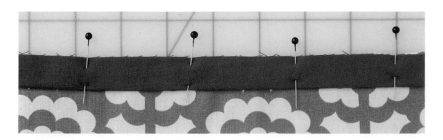

**4** Press the seam toward the ruffled hem band. Topstitch close to the seam.

**5** Sew gathering stitches along the raw edge of the ruffled hem band within the ½″ seam allowance.

**6** Adjust the gathers to fit the bottom skirt edge. Carefully pin the ruffled hem band to the bottom edge of the skirt with right sides facing. Stitch together and press the seam toward the apron. Topstitch close to the seam.

## Prepare the Skirt

**1** Sew a ¼″ hem on both sides of the apron skirt (see Hemming, page 123). **A**

**2** Sew gathering stitches on the top edge of the skirt. Pull the gathering threads until the skirt measures 24″ across.

**3** Mark the center at the top of the skirt and the center of the waistband bottom.

**4** With right sides facing, match center markings and pin the waistband to the skirt top. Adjust the gathers and stitch. Press the seam toward the waistband.

### NOTE
Approximately 2″ of waistband should overhang each side to allow for waist size adjustment. **B**

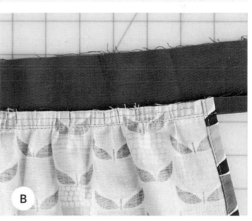

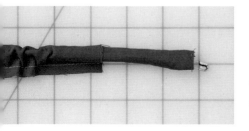

## Prepare the Neck Tie

**1** Fold the neck tie strip lengthwise with right sides together and pin. Sew down the length of the strip using a ¼″ seam.

**2** Turn the tube right side out by pinning a large safety pin to an end and carefully pushing it through until it comes out the other end.

**3** Press the neck tie flat with the seam to a side. Fold each raw edge to the inside and press. Sew the ends with a narrow seam or hand stitch closed.

## Prepare the Bodice

**1** Hem the sides of the bodice in the same manner as the skirt.

**2** To make the neck tie casing, fold under the top edge ¼″ and press. Fold under another 1″ and press. **A**

**3** Pin the casing in place and stitch close to the inner edge. Thread the neck tie through the casing. **B**

**4** Sew gathering stitches along the bottom edge of the bodice. Mark the center and pull the gathers until the bodice is approximately 15″ across. Make sure that the gathers are evenly distributed.

**5** Mark the center point of the waistband at the top. With right sides facing, pin the bodice to the waistband, matching the 2 center markings. **C**

**6** Stitch the bodice to the waistband using a ⅜″ seam. This seam is to secure these 2 pieces prior to attaching the waistband lining. Press the seam flat.

**7** Turn under a long edge of the waistband lining ½″ and press. Pin the raw edge of the waistband lining to the waistband, with right sides facing, sandwiching the bodice between them. Stitch them together using a ½″ seam. **D**

**8** Press the waistband lining down toward the skirt. **E**

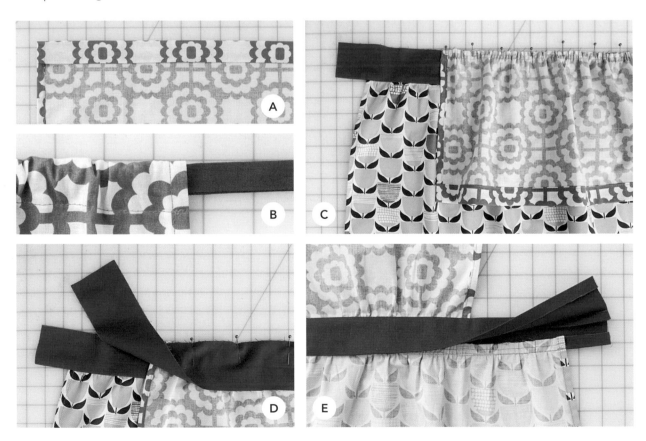

## Prepare the Waist Ties

**1** Sew a ¼˝ hem along 1 long edge of a tie.

**2** To make a point at the end of the tie, fold the end diagonally, right sides facing, matching the raw edges. Stitch a seam ½˝ from the edge.

**3** Turn the point right side out. Hem the remaining long raw edge and topstitch the pointed end.

**4** Repeat for the second tie.

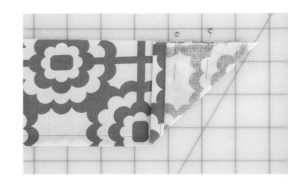

## Assemble the Apron

**1** Trim the waistband and waistband lining so that it extends ½˝ beyond the skirt.

**2** Place the waistband flat with the lining up. Pin a waist tie to the end of the waistband, matching raw edges. Pin a small pleat in the middle of the tie to match the width of the waistband. Baste the tie to waistband (see Basting, page 121). **A**

**3** Fold the waistband lining down over the tie, keeping both waistband pieces right sides facing. This creates a sandwich with the tie in the middle. Pin in place.

**4** Stitch the raw ends of the waistband. Make sure the seam is even with the finished edge of the skirt. **B**

**5** Trim the seam to ¼˝, trim the corners, turn right side out, and press.

**6** Repeat for the second side.

**7** Pin the folded edge of the waistband lining to the skirt, barely overlapping the seam. Hand baste the waistband lining to the skirt, if necessary. Topstitch around the entire waistband. **C**

# CHIFFON AND LACE SKIRT

by Disney Powless

Mix vintage lace with dreamy chiffon to make this beautiful, romantic skirt. If you don't already have a stash of your grandmother's vintage laces, we suggest keeping an eye out at antique stores and estate sales.

# MEET THE DESIGNER

Disney Powless is a DIY-type wife and mommy from Washington State. She has had work published in many magazines and online, but her favorite place to share her ideas is on her popular craft blog, where she shares not only craft and sewing tutorials but a sunny outlook on life. She also loves photography, thrifting, homeschooling her daughter, working with foster children, and helping her husband behind the scenes in his preaching ministry. Follow Disney at *Ruffles & Stuff* (rufflesandstuff.com).

---

**Finished length:** 31″ long

**Fabrics:** Ivory chiffon tricot from Fabric.com and vintage lace pieces

---

## FABRIC REQUIREMENTS

*Note: You may want to calculate the sizes of your pieces (see Cutting) before you buy your fabric.*

- **Ivory or white chiffon:** 2–5 yards (yardage depends on fabric width and size of skirt)

- **Nonsheer lining fabric:** 1–2 yards

- **Matching lace:** 4 different kinds (Each piece of lace should be twice your waist measurement.)

## Additional supplies

- **2″-wide elastic:** enough to fit comfortably around your waist

## CUTTING

### From the lining fabric, cut:

1 rectangle approximately 22″ long and twice your waist measurement in width

*Note: If your lining fabric is not wide enough, cut 2 pieces 22″ long and your waist measurement plus ½″ in width and sew them together at one side.*

### From the chiffon, cut:

4 rectangles that are the same width as your lining and 30″, 27½″, 25″, and 22½″ long

### From the 2″-wide elastic, cut:

1 piece that fits your waist snugly but not tight

A

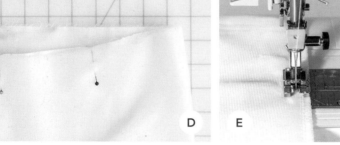

B

C

# Sewing

*Seam allowances are ½″ unless otherwise noted.*

**1** Sew together the ends of the elastic to make a circle; then sew the seam edges flat. **A**

**2** Select and sew lace to the bottom edge of each sheer panel. If your lace is different widths, you may want to trim the chiffon pieces so that they layer evenly after the lace is sewn on. **B**

**3** Pin together the sides of the lining with right sides facing and sew to make a circle. Repeat for each sheer panel. Sew a ¼″ hem on the lining (see Hemming, page 123). **C**

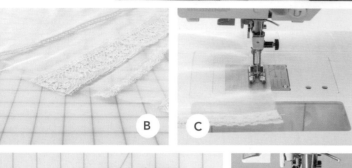

D

E

**4** Assemble the skirt by pinning together all of the pieces at the waist—place the lining on the inside and longest sheer panel next, ending with the shortest sheer panel. **D**

**5** Serge or zigzag stitch all layers together along the top edge. Then, with the needle placed just below the serged or zigzagged stitches, sew a gathering stitch to gather the top of the skirt until it is slightly larger than the waistband (see Gathering, page 122). **E**

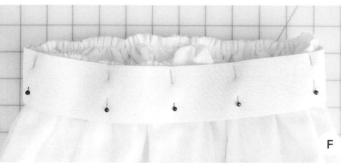

F

**6** Pin the skirt to the waistband with the fullness evenly distributed. The waistband should be upside down over the skirt with the edges flush. **F**

**7** Sew the skirt to the waistband, gently stretching the elastic as you go to match the width of the skirt. Use a narrow zigzag stitch so that it will stretch with the waistband (see Stretch Stitching, page 126). **G**

G

**8** Fold up the waistband and you're done.

# BELLA POUCH

by Bonnie Rosales

This sweet little pouch is just big enough to grab and go when you want to carry only the essentials. It's such a versatile shape. It includes an inside pocket and a wrist strap.

## MEET THE DESIGNER

Bonnie Rosales is a stay-at-home mom. She is happily married and has a four-year-old son, whom she recently started homeschooling. Family means everything to her. She taught herself how to sew about two years ago and has been learning new things ever since. She loves to read, write, and create pretty things. See what Bonnie is up to at *Pink Stitches* (pinkxstitches.blogspot.com).

**Finished size:** 6½˝ wide × 5½˝ tall × 2½˝ deep

**Fabric:** Carnaby Street by Pat Bravo from Art Gallery Fabrics; hardware from Tantalizing Stitches

## FABRIC REQUIREMENTS

*A fat quarter is a piece of fabric that measures 18˝ × 22˝.*

- **Coordinating quilting-weight cotton:** 3 fat quarters

- **Lightweight fusible interfacing (such as Pellon 906F):** ½ yard

- **Cotton batting:** ½ yard

*Additional supplies*

- **Magnetic snap**

- **Small lobster clasp with a ½˝ opening**

- **½˝ D-ring**

## CUTTING

✂ *Patterns are on pullout page P2.*

*From a fat quarter, cut:*

2 using pattern A for the exterior body

1 using pattern B for the exterior flap

*From another fat quarter, cut:*

2 using pattern A for the body lining

1 using pattern B for the flap lining

*From the last fat quarter, cut:*

2 rectangles 6˝ × 5˝ for the pocket

1 strip 14½˝ × 2˝ for the wristlet strap

1 strip 2½˝ × 2˝ for the D-ring tab

*From the interfacing, cut:*

2 using pattern A for the body

2 using pattern B for the flap

*From the batting, cut:*

4 using pattern A

2 using pattern B

# Sewing

*Seam allowances are ¼″ unless otherwise noted.*

## Sew the Wristlet Strap, D-Ring Tab, and Pocket

**1** Fold and press the wristlet strap and the D-ring tab pieces in half lengthwise. Open up and bring the raw edges to the center fold and press again. Fold the tab in half and press again to make a ½″-wide strip. Set the wristlet strap aside.

**2** Topstitch the D-ring tab along the open side and set aside. **A**

**3** Place the pocket pieces together with right sides facing. Sew along all 4 sides, leaving a 3″ opening in the center of the bottom (one of

the longer sides). Trim the corners, turn the pocket inside out, and press.

**4** Topstitch 2 rows of stitching along the top edge of the pocket. **B**

**5** Center the pocket on a lining piece about ¾″ from the top. Pin it in place and topstitch along the sides and bottom. **C**

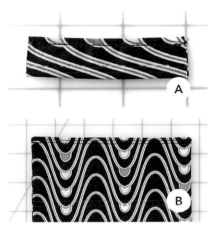

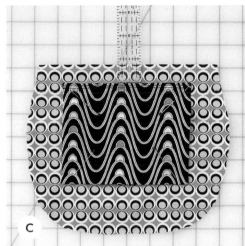

## Sew the Body

**1** Fuse the interfacing to the wrong side of both exterior body pieces. Place the body batting pieces on the wrong side of each exterior and lining piece.

**2** Make a mark for the magnetic snap on an exterior body piece, centered 2″ down from the top edge. Insert the female side of a magnetic

snap at the marking (see Inserting a Magnetic Snap, page 124). **A**

**3** Transfer the dart markings from the pattern to the wrong side of each body piece and sew each of the darts as marked. Be careful not to sew over the pocket on the lining piece. **B**

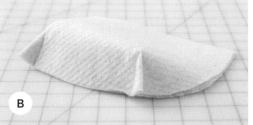

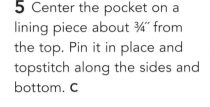

**4** Slip the D-ring through the tab piece and pin it between the exterior pieces about 1½″ from the top of the main exterior piece. Pin or baste the tab in place. **C**

**5** Place together the 2 body exterior pieces with right sides facing and pin. Make sure to line up the darts. **D**

**6** Sew along the curve, leaving the top open. Clip the curve and turn the pouch right side out (see Clipping and Notching, page 122). Press. The D-ring tab should be facing out. Set the pouch aside. **E**

**7** Repeat Steps 5 and 6 with the body lining pieces. Leave a 3″ opening on the bottom of the lining for turning later. Set the lining aside.

## Prepare the Flap

**1** Fuse the flap interfacing to the wrong side of each fabric flap piece. Layer the flap batting on top of the interfacing. Each flap piece should now have 3 layers.

**2** Make a mark for the magnetic snap on the flap lining centered and 1¼″ up from the curved edge. Insert the male side of the magnetic snap at the marking (see Inserting a Magnetic Snap, page 124). **A**

**3** Place together the flap pieces with right sides facing and pin. **B**

**4** Sew along the curve, leaving the top side open. Clip the curves. Turn the flap right sides out and press. Topstitch ¼″ from the curved edge. **C**

**5** Center the flap on the back of the assembled pouch and pin. Make sure the D-ring is on the right side. The magnetic snap should be facing you. Pin or baste the flap to the body. **D**

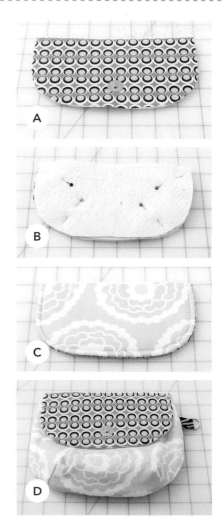

# Final Pouch Construction

**1** Place the assembled exterior pouch inside the lining pouch. The lining pouch should still be inside out. Make sure the inside pocket is facing the flap. Pin the lining in place. Sew along the top edge of the pouch. **A**

**2** Turn the pouch right side out using the opening at the bottom of the lining. Slipstitch the lining closed (see Slipstitching, page 126).

**3** Press the top seam firmly to reduce some of the bulk. Topstitch ¼″ from the top seam. **B**

## Prepare the Strap

**1** Slip the lobster clasp onto the long folded wrist strap piece. Place together both ends of the strap with right sides facing and stitch it in place. Press the seam open. **A**

**2** Fold the strap back to the way it was and topstitch along the entire strap. **B**

**3** Pinch the wrist strap together, positioning the seam at the swivel clasp, and stitch to keep it in place. Attach the strap to the pouch and you're done! **C**

# MINI DRESDEN COIN PURSE

by Amy B. Friend

This adorable little coin purse is just the thing to throw in your purse to hold your coins, cash, and credit cards. Stitch one up for a friend and you'll have the perfect little gift.

# MEET THE DESIGNER

Amy is a pattern designer, quilter, sewer, and sometimes printmaker. She has been blogging about her creations since 2009. She enjoys a wide variety of crafts, but fabric and printmaking have been her long-standing interests. Currently, she is particularly enjoying designing paper-pieced patterns and modern quiltmaking. She is the co-founder the Seacoast Modern Quilt Guild in coastal New England. Amy has a bachelor of arts degree in art/art history from Bates College and completed her master's course work in art history at the University of Delaware. She worked as a curator of fine arts collections prior to staying at home with her three children. She was recently able to dabble in museum work while partnering with Berene Campbell to install the *To Boston with Love* exhibit at the Museum of Fine Arts in Boston. Visit Amy at *During Quiet Time* (duringquiettime.blogspot.com).

---

**Finished size:** 6¾″ × 5″

**Fabrics:** Bijoux by Bari J. from Art Gallery Fabrics and Quilter's Linen from Robert Kaufman

---

## FABRIC REQUIREMENTS

- **For exterior:** ¼ yard cotton solid

- **For lining:** ¼ yard cotton

- **For the Dresden blades:** small pieces of fabric in as many different prints as desired

### Additional supplies

- **Nylon zipper:** 7″ or longer

- **Small scraps of double-sided fusible web (such as HeatnBond Fusible Feather Lite adhesive)**

- **Heavyweight interfacing (such as HeatnBond Non-Woven Craft Fusible Firm interfacing):** ¼ yard

- **Needle and thread**

## CUTTING

✂ *Patterns are on pullout page P4.*

*From the exterior fabric, cut:*

2 pieces using the Purse Body pattern

*From the lining fabric, cut:*

2 pieces using the Purse Body pattern

2 rectangles 1½″ × 2½″ for the zipper tabs

*From the small print fabrics, cut:*

11 pieces using the Dresden Blade pattern

1 square 2″ × 2″ for the Dresden center

*From the double-sided fusible web, cut:*

1 piece using the Dresden Center pattern

1 piece using the Dresden Body pattern

*From heavyweight interfacing, cut:*

2 pieces using the Purse Body pattern

# Sewing

*Seam allowances are ¼″ unless otherwise noted.*

## Appliqué the Dresden Plate

**1** Sew the Dresden blades together using a scant ¼″ seam. Don't worry about the bulk at the center point because it will be trimmed away. **A**

**2** Center the piece of fusible web on the square for the center and fuse. Leave the paper on the web. Trim your fabric about ¼″ beyond the fusible web along the curve. **B**

**3** Cut a piece of cereal box or other cardboard the same size as the Dresden center template. Place cardboard on the back of the fabric and use a piece of foil to help fold the fabric around the cardboard. Press the edges firmly. Let the foil cool completely. **C**

A

> ### Amy's Tip
> You may want to fussy cut your Dresden center fabric for added interest.

B

**4** Remove the foil and peel away the fusible web paper. Fuse the folded edges carefully in place with the tip of an iron. **D**

**5** Trim away the bulk in the center of the Dresden blades and pin the center in place. Carefully hand stitch the center to the Dresden blades with invisible stitches to complete the Dresden plate. **E**

**6** Apply the Dresden body piece of fusible web to the wrong side of the Dresden plate. Center this piece on the exterior front of the purse and fuse. Using a tight, narrow zigzag stitch and coordinating thread, stitch along the outside edge of the Dresden plate.

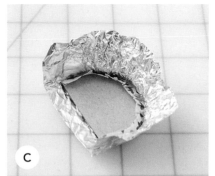

## Prepare the Zipper

**1** Create the zipper tabs by ironing the short ends under ¼″ and then folding it in half. **A**

**2** With the zipper closed, trim it a bit shorter than the top of the Dresden purse, to about 5½″.

**3** Slip each end of the zipper into a zipper tab to make the final length of the zipper piece equal to the width of the top of the purse. Sew close to the pressed fold. Trim the sides of the zipper tabs to match the width of the zipper. **B**

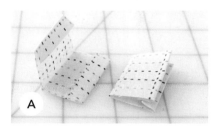

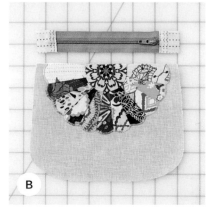

# Assemble the Purse

**1** Place the exterior front piece right side up. Place the zipper facedown on top, followed by the lining fabric right side down. Stitch along the upper edge using a zipper foot. **A**

**2** Fold the lining to the back, press, and topstitch along the upper edge. **B**

**3.** Place the exterior back fabric right side up, followed by the section just made facing down, then the lining fabric with right side down. Stitch across the upper edge. **C**

**4** Fold back the lining and press. Topstitch along the upper edge. **D**

**5** Flip the pieces around so that the exterior fabrics face each other and the lining fabrics face each other. Leave the zipper partially open. Stitch all the way around, leaving an opening at the bottom of the lining for turning. **E**

**6** Turn the purse through the opening. Slipstitch the opening closed and press the purse (see Slipstitching, page 126).

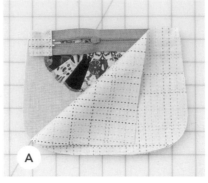

A

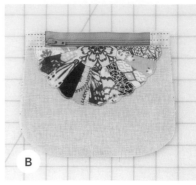

B

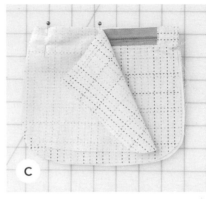

C

D

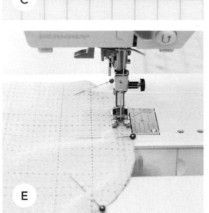

E

# FOXY SMARTPHONE COZY

by Lisa Cox

Sized to fit most smartphones, the Foxy Smartphone Cozy is constructed from thick industrial felt. It will keep your phone well protected and make it easy to find in your handbag. A colorful felt fox appliqué adds some fun. With an elastic strap in the back to hold your earbuds, these covers can be quickly constructed and are the perfect gift for technology lovers.

## MEET THE DESIGNER

Lisa Cox is an occupational therapist by day and an avid sewist, quilter, and crafter by night at her home in Perth, Australia. Lisa loves to travel and has lived in Australia, the United States, France, and Norway. She is inspired by craft techniques that she discovers on her travels. Lisa can usually be found in her craft room or kitchen, working on her latest project.

Lisa's sewing and quilting designs have been published in the books *Fabric-by-Fabric One-Yard Wonders*, *Craft Hope*, *Pretty Little Presents*, and *Sweet Nothings*, as well as in several magazines including *Stitch*, *Handmade*, *Australian Homespun*, and *Quilting Arts Magazine*.

Lisa collaborates on a blog with her daughter, Sarah. They love to share their creative tutorials, fresh project ideas, and delicious recipes. You can follow their sewing, crafting, and baking adventures at *A Spoonful of Sugar* (aspoonfulofsugardesigns.com).

---

**Finished size:** 5¼″ × 3½″ (*Be sure to measure your phone before starting and make any necessary adjustments.*)

**Fabric:** Wool felt from A Child's Dream Come True. Ribbon from Renaissance Ribbons.

## CUTTING

*From the industrial felt, cut:*

1 rectangle 10½″ × 3½″ for the cozy

## FABRIC REQUIREMENTS

- **For the cozy:** ⅛ yard industrial felt, 3mm thick

- **For the fox:** small pieces of orange and white 1mm wool felt

### Additional supplies

- **Paper-backed fusible appliqué web** (such as Steam-A-Seam or Wonder-Under)

- **1 small black button:** ¼″ diameter

- **2 small black seed beads**

- **½″-wide black elastic:** 4½″

- **Printed tape or ribbon:** 2″ long × ½″–1″ wide

- **Jeans (heavy-duty) needle for sewing machine**

- **Small quilt binding clips**

- **Embroidery needle**

**NOTE**

If you can't find industrial felt, try 2 or 3 layers of standard 1mm felt, or use 1 layer of 1mm wool felt for a slightly roomier, more flexible cozy.

# Sewing

✂ *Patterns are on pullout page P1.*

*Seam allowances are ¼″ unless otherwise noted.*

**1** Trace the fox appliqué shapes onto the paper backing of the fusible web and cut around the shapes, leaving at least a ¼″ allowance. Note that the tail is reversed so that when you peel off the paper and turn it over to fuse it, it will be right. Fuse the appliqué web to the wrong side of the appropriate color wool felt, following manufacturer's directions— use white for the head and tail and orange for the body, face/ears, and base of the tail. Cut the wool felt into the fox shapes using the traced lines as a guide. **A**

**2** Peel the paper backing off of the orange shapes. Place the orange part of the tail on top of the white tail. Place the orange part of the face on top of the white face. Iron to fuse the pieces in place. **B**

**3** Peel the paper backing from the rest the fox appliqué pieces and place them on the front of the cozy, approximately 1″ down from the top edge. Iron to fuse the pieces in place. **C**

**4** Using the black topstitching thread and a jeans needle in the sewing machine, stitch the felt pieces in place. Stitch around the fox appliqué twice. Try to avoid stitching on the same line to give it a sketchy appearance.

**5** Stitch the button in place for the nose of the fox. Stitch the seed beads in place for the eyes.

**6** Fold the cozy in half and hold the sides in place using the small binding clips. Fold the piece of ribbon in half and position it in the left-hand seam, ¾″ up from the bottom fold. **D**

**7** Position the elastic 1⅞″ down from the top edge on the back of the cozy, with the ends tucked into the seam. Stitch both sides of the cozy using a coordinating thread, securing the elastic and the ribbon tab in the seam as you sew. Backstitch at the beginning and end. **E**

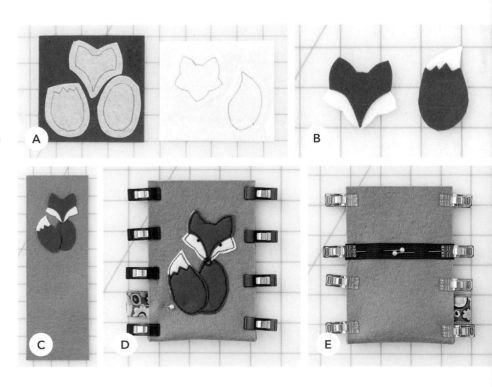

## MAKING CONTINUOUS BIAS TRIM

### Prepare a Continuous Bias Strip

*Seam allowances are ¼˝ unless otherwise noted.*

**1** Start with a square of fabric. Cut the square into 2 triangles. **A**

**2** Place a triangle on top of the other with right sides facing, matching up 2 of the shorter edges. Pin and stitch. **B**

**3** Open up the fabric and you have a trapezoid. Press the seam open. Starting at the bottom, use a clear ruler to draw horizontal lines the desired distance apart until you reach the top. You may have to trim some fabric off the top if there is not enough left for the size strip you want. **C**

**4** Fold the trapezoid with right sides facing, putting the short ends together. Don't match the strips up exactly—offset them by a strip. A strip will hang off each end. **D**

> ### Caroline's Tip
> The lines on the fabric should meet at the ¼˝ seam allowance, not at the raw edge. This means the hand-drawn lines will be offset by about ¼˝ at the raw edges.

**5** Sew together the ends. **E**

**6** Press the seam open. Cut along the lines you drew and you have a long bias strip! **F**

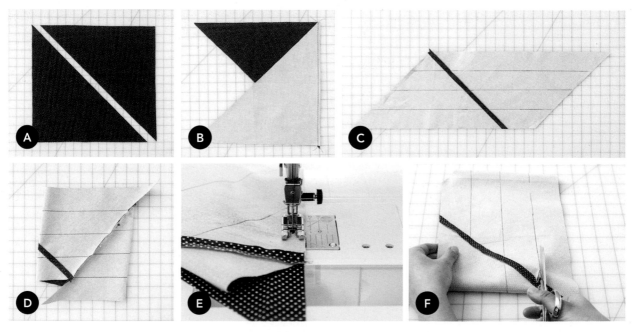

## Making Single- or Double-Fold Trim

### Single-Fold Bias Trim

Fold the bias strip in half, wrong sides facing. Open it up and fold the edges to the center. Press. **G**

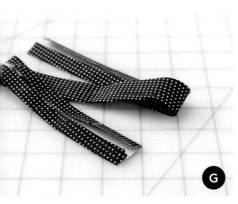

Alternatively, use a bias tape maker. Insert an end of your bias strip into the wide end of the bias tape maker. Use a pin to help push it all the way through, if necessary. Press the bias tape as it comes out the other end. **H**

Single-fold bias trim is used on the Saturday Night Tunic (page 76) neckline and sleeves.

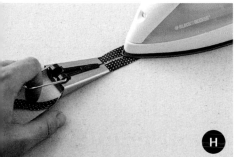

### Double-Fold Bias Trim

Fold single-fold bias trim in half once more (down the center) and press. **I**

Double-fold bias trim is used on the Quilting Bee Dress (page 27) neckline and sleeves and for the pocket trim on the Venna Tote (page 20).

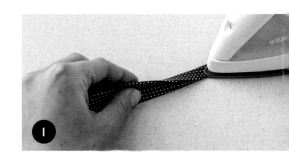

## BASTING

*Use a basting stitch to hold multiple layers of fabric together until they are stitched permanently.*

**1** Set the sewing machine to the longest stitch length or the basting stitch (if available).

**2** Sew the items together as directed. Backstitch as desired.

# GATHERING

*Use this technique to create ruffles or ruching as in the Retro Urban Apron (page 98).*

**1** Adjust the stitch length to the longest stitch and reduce the top thread tension slightly. Sew 1 or 2 rows of gathering stitches within the seam allowance. Do not backstitch and remember to leave the threads long.

**2** Gently pull on the bobbin thread to gather the material to the desired width. If 2 rows are sewn, pull both bobbin threads at the same time for best results.

### Sarah's Tip

For getting perfect gathers that won't wiggle around as you sew: Sew a row of gathering stitches on each side of the seamline. Arrange the gathers as desired and sew between the 2 lines. Then remove the visible gathering thread that is outside the seam allowance.

# CLIPPING AND NOTCHING

*Note: When clipping and notching, be careful not to cut into the stitching that holds together the seam.*

**Clipping** a seam allowance is often used on inside curved seams such as armholes or necklines. The clips allow the seam allowance to spread out so it lies smooth and flat without puckering.

**Notches** are cut into outward curves to remove bulk when a seam allowance is turned inside out.

**Corners** are trimmed to remove bulk.

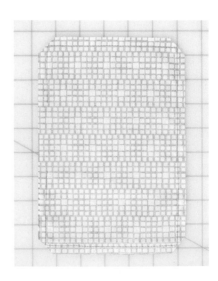

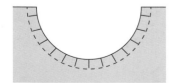

# MAKING BUTTONHOLES

If your machine doesn't make automatic buttonholes, the following is an easy way to make them:

**1** Measure around the button with a narrow piece of ribbon. Flatten this loop of ribbon and measure the doubled length.

**2** Mark the buttonhole on the fabric the length you just measured.

**3** Set the sewing machine to a wide zigzag stitch, about 4.0mm, and a very short stitch length.

**4** Stitch with the wide zigzag at an end of the buttonhole mark for about 6 stitches.

**5** Reset the stitch width to about 1.5mm and stitch down a side of the buttonhole mark.

**6** Switch back to the wide zigzag and stitch the other end of the buttonhole.

**7** Reset the stitch width back to 1.5mm and stitch back up the other side of the buttonhole mark, keeping the line visible between the 2 rows of stitches. Backstitch to end stitching and carefully trim threads.

**8** With small sharp scissors, carefully cut the buttonhole opening. You can put a pin across each end to prevent cutting into the end stitches.

# HEMMING

*Hemming is a way to finish a raw edge. When sewing garments, the suggested hem allowance may always be adjusted for the most flattering length for you!*

**1** Fold the raw edge of the fabric toward the wrong side of the fabric ¼″ and press. **A**

**2** Fold the edge to the wrong side a second time the amount specified for the hem and press. **B**

**3** Stitch close to the inner folded edge. When the thread closely matches the fabric, the hem won't be noticed. If you have a serger, you can serge the edge instead of making the first fold, and then continue at Step 2. **C**

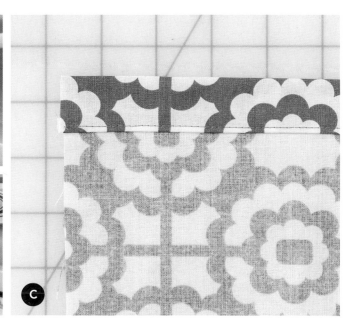

# HEMMING WITH A DOUBLE NEEDLE

*Use double-needle hemming on knit fabrics because it stretches and prevents thread breakage.*

**1** Press the raw edge of the hemline to the inside ½˝. Finishing the edge is optional because knit fabrics do not fray. **A**

**2** Put 2 spools of thread on your sewing machine. You can use a filled bobbin for the second spool if you don't have 2 spools of the same color. **B**

**3** Insert the double needle into your sewing machine and thread each eye, 1 at a time. Both threads should pass through all the usual tension guides.

**4** Sew on the outside of the project, ½˝ from folded edge. Make sure that your stitching catches the raw edge underneath. Backstitch as usual at the beginning and ending of your stitching as needed. **C**

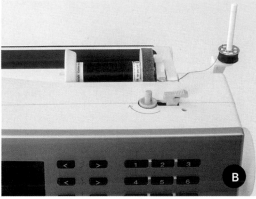

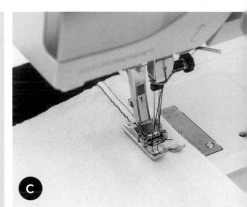

# INSERTING A MAGNETIC SNAP

*When inserting a magnetic snap into lightweight fabric, if your fabric is not already interfaced, it is best to fuse a small square of interfacing or fusible fleece at the area of insertion. This will help prevent the snap from pulling out during use. This example has interfacing already fused to the back of the fabric.*

**1** Mark the magnetic snap placement as instructed in the pattern.

**2** Place the metal disk that came with the magnetic snap over the center of the placement mark. Draw lines inside the slits on each side of the center. **A**

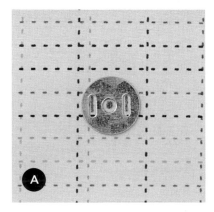

**3** Using sharp scissors or a seam ripper, cut small slits along the lines. Slide the prongs of the snap through the slits. **B**

**4** Place a small circle of felt, cardboard, or plastic onto the prongs to prevent the metal disk from cutting into the fabric during use. Then place the metal disk over the prongs. Flexible plastic shelf liner is pictured here. **C**

**5** Close the prongs by folding them outward. If the prongs are too hard to bend with your fingers, use the handle of a screwdriver or scissors to bend them down. Repeat for the opposite side of the magnetic snap. **D**

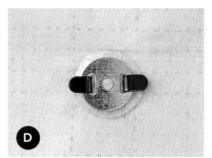

# SHIRRING

*Use shirring to make rows of gathers. Results may vary, depending on the brand of your sewing machine.*

**1** Hand wind elastic thread in the bobbin with only light tension. Increase the stitch length setting on the sewing machine.

**2** With elastic thread on the bottom and regular thread on top, sew a row of shirring in the desired location using a long stitch length. Be sure to backstitch at the beginning and end of each line of shirring.

**3** When shirring around the body of an item, such as the Boho Maxi Dress (page 58) or the Saturday Night Tunic (page 76), there is no need to trim threads between lines. Simply backstitch over the start of the finished row, lift the presser foot, and shift your project so you can start the next row. **A**

## *Caroline's Tips*

- Gently pull the fabric smooth as you go around rows 2 through the end.

- After shirring, apply steam from your iron to shrink the thread and tighten the gathers.

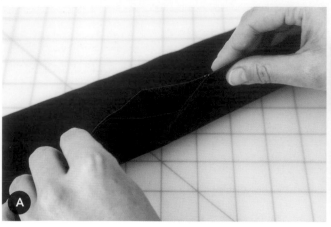

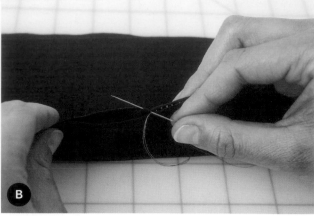

## SLIPSTITCHING

*Use a slipstitch to close the lining of purses and other items with enclosed seams.*

**1** Press the raw edges to the inside and clearly define the edges to be sewn together. **A**

**2** Using a hand needle and matching thread, sew the opening closed with hidden stitches. The contrasting thread in the photo is for illustrative purposes only. **B**

## STRETCH STITCHING

*Use a stretch stitch on knit fabrics to prevent the thread from breaking when the fabric stretches.*

Your sewing machine may include a stretch stitch, which looks kind of like a lightning bolt or a widely spaced, skinny zigzag stitch. If your machine doesn't have a stretch stitch, use a narrow (0.5mm–1.0mm) zigzag stitch.

## TOPSTITCHING

*Topstitching is sewing a row of stitches on the top or right side of the fabric. A slightly heavier thread may be used for the top thread to give it a little more pop, as seen in the Topstitched Belt (page 81).*

Adjust the machine's stitch length so it is a bit longer than usual (2.5mm–3.0mm). Stitch on the right side of your project, parallel to the seam or edge, as directed.

**STRETCH STITCHING**

**TOPSTITCHING**

# About the Authors

## Caroline Fairbanks-Critchfield

Caroline comes from a family of artists and computer geeks. Of course, the artists go back further than the computer geeks, who started with her dad. Her mom taught her to sew, while her dad taught her to use one of the first home computers ever released: the Apple computer with the green screen.

She sewed her way through elementary and high school, and then squeezed in more time to sew while studying Russian language and literature at Brigham Young University. A brief internship at the Boston Museum of Fine Arts (under the tutelage of her great-uncle, who was a curator) increased her love for textiles.

Sometime after her first little girl was born, Caroline realized that sewing and computers went together. She started her first sewing blog to share and show off her projects, and soon she began designing patterns that featured only one pattern piece.

Now, by happy accident or not, her home has become one where the creative spirit runs free. Raw materials come in; and robots, pillows, and cute things to wear go out. Caroline's sewing is second only to her four children and husband. You can see what she's making right now at *SewCanShe* (sewcanshe.com/blog).

## Sarah Markos

Sarah is a fabric addict with a love of all things crafty. She inherited this passion from her mother and grandmother, who also loved to sew. She grew up in a home where handmade gifts were cherished and creativity was encouraged, resulting in doll dresses, church dresses, prom dresses, wedding dresses, and countless other sewing projects. She learned to sew at an early age but really learned to love it as a teenager, when she took apart her favorite pair of pants and used it as a pattern to make a new pair.

She has honed her sewing skills, making endless Halloween costumes and items for her children, unique Christmas and baby gifts for friends, and decor for her home. She started designing and sewing handbags to sell at local holiday fairs as a way to use up her ever-growing fabric stash. She blogs about her sewing adventures at *Blue Susan Makes*.

Sarah lives in West Melbourne, Florida, with her husband and four children. She has a bachelor's degree in nursing from Brigham Young University and enjoys telling gory stories from her life as an operating room nurse. She also loves being a mom, running, reading to her children, refinishing furniture, and teaching people to sew. Visit her at *Blue Susan Makes* (bluesusanmakes.blogspot.com).

# Where to Find It Online

**NOTE**

Some of these listings are for fabric manufacturers that only sell wholesale. Use their sites to look at fabric collections and to find a retail store that sells their fabrics.

## Fabrics

A Child's Dream Come True (felt)
**achildsdream.com**

Andover Fabrics
**andoverfabrics.com**

Art Gallery Fabrics
**artgalleryfabrics.com**

Dear Stella
**dearstelladesign.com**

Fat Quarter Shop
**fatquartershop.com**

Girl Charlee (knit fabrics)
**girlcharlee.com**

Michael Miller Fabrics
**michaelmillerfabrics.com**

Robert Kaufman Fabrics
**robertkaufman.com**

The Fabric Fairy (knit fabrics)
**thefabricfairy.com**

Westminster Fabrics
**westminsterfabrics.com**

## Notions and Findings

BagPurseFrames
**etsy.com/shop/bagpurseframes**

fast2fuse
**ctpub.com**

Fire Mountain Gems and Beads
**firemountaingems.com**

PurseSuppliesRUs
**etsy.com/shop/PurseSuppliesRUs**

Renaissance Ribbons
**retail.renaissanceribbons.com**

Tantalizing Stitches
**etsy.com/shop/tantalizingstitches**

Soft & Stable
**byannie.com**

Zipit
**etsy.com/shop/zipit**